THE COMPASSIONATE
SIDE OF DIVORCE

THE COMPASSIONATE SIDE OF DIVORCE

by

C. S. LOVETT, M.A., B.D., D.D.

Director of Personal Christianity

author of
SOUL-WINNING MADE EASY
DEALING WITH THE DEVIL
WITNESSING MADE EASY
JESUS WANTS YOU WELL!

Illustrated by Marjorie Lovett
and Linda Lovett

Cover photo by J. Richard Lee

PERSONAL CHRISTIANITY
Baldwin Park, California

Distributed to the book trade exclusively by
Fleming H. Revell Company
Old Tappan, New Jersey

To
Marjorie

My partner in the adventure of Christian marriage for more than 32 years.

PRINTED IN THE UNITED STATES OF AMERICA
by
EL CAMINO PRESS
LA VERNE, CA 91750

CONTENTS

ANOINTED FOR READING?

A single verse unlocks the treasure of this book.

"For the Lord seeth not as a man seeth: For man looketh on the outward appearance, but the Lord looketh on the heart" (1 Sam. 16:7).

You must lay hold of the meaning of that verse. Only then will you be ready to measure what you read. Few books require the anointing of the Holy Spirit for a proper understanding. This one does. Those with God's anointing will view the wonder of His grace in the . . .

TOLERATION PRINCIPLE.

The author does not hold these things to be true simply because he has written them, but only as the Holy Spirit bears witness to them. If you cannot find God's testimony as you read, set the book aside. If you find His blessed witness, then do as the Apostle Paul begs . . . "enlarge your hearts . . ." and extend your tender grace toward those who are casualties of the marriage program.

FOR COUNSELORS ONLY!

"All right, Mr. McHenry, here's what I want you to do. Don't make your decision right away. Take this book with you and read it before you come to see me next Tuesday. It will help you think through your situation and come to a decision that will please the Lord."

The book that counselor presented to his client is the same as the one you are reading right now, **The Compassionate Side of Divorce.** The truths in it are powerful. It sets forth scriptural principles that a person can apply to his own situation and see exactly what to do and where he stands with the Lord in the matter. This can be of tremendous help when a person is facing a divorce or is in a state of confusion because of having gone through a divorce. It shows born-again believers how to THINK THROUGH their situation before the Lord and come step-by-step to the right decision.

"All right, Mr. McHenry, take this book with you and read it."

This, of course, makes it a terrific tool for counselors. It saves them hours of valuable time which they might otherwise have to spend in trying to explain God's feelings in a divorce situation. Not only that, it gives the Holy Spirit a chance to work with your client when he's all alone with his thoughts and move on his heart to make him desire God's will. It's a great blessing to have such a tool and to be able to put specific help in the hands of those coming to you for divorce counsel. There's another side to it, though. When you have powerful tools that really help people, the devil can use them too.

SO SOME CAUTION IS NEEDED

Naturally you would not place a book in a client's hands until you had first read it yourself. When you read this one, you'll see at once that some people should be warned about it. Who? Those looking for an ESCAPE from marriage. A lot of immature Christians run from marriage. They won't honestly face up to their responsibilities and when the pressures mount, the first thing they think of — is divorce. If you have been counseling for some time, you've undoubtedly had some of these people in your office.

Unfortunately this book can be twisted by those who simply want out of their marriages. They won't hesitate to pervert the principles and use them to justify filing for a divorce. Those tired of their mates and wanting to try someone else, will be tempted to use this book as grounds for pleasing their flesh. But of course, God has the same problem. People take His book, the Bible, and twist it to suit their preferences. There are plenty of Christians who bend and pervert the Word of God to vindicate their actions. I say that, so you won't feel too badly when people use this book to satisfy their carnal desires. You simply have the same problem God has.

When it is obvious that you are dealing with a client whose heart is set on getting a divorce regardless of God's will, you should **warn him** that the principles in this book can be employed as justification for satisfying the desires of the flesh. Your caution might go like this:

"I feel I should warn you, Mr. Evans, that it is

possible to take the principles you'll find in this book and use them to justify your plans for a divorce. Don't do it. Don't let Satan deceive you into insisting on your own will. As you read, ask the Holy Spirit to show you God's will and then be ready to do it. If you will adopt that kind of an attitude, then this book can give you the kind of help you really need. But if you insist on using it to justify doing your own thing . . . God will let you do it. And you'll reap the consequences."

WHEN THE PERSON IS GENUINELY SINCERE

Let's suppose you've been counseling a lady who is married to a cruel and unreasonable man. She's been his slave for years, suffering terribly at his hands. Her first thought, in coming to see you, was to find some way to win this man to the Lord. And of course, you go along with that. You always try to save marriages by bringing Jesus into them. That's the first step. And so for the past few months you have been advising her as to the different strategies a wife can use to win her husband to Christ without actually preaching to him. This lady is a godly Christian and knows the Word of God forbids wives to preach to their husbands (I Peter 3:1,2).

NOTE. I would like to mention that my book, **Unequally Yoked Wives** can be a tremendous help to those counseling women living with unsaved husbands. It is an effective plan for using a wife's SUBMISSION to put a powerful squeeze on her husband. Many women submit to their mates because the Word tells them to. But that's as far as it goes. Their husbands simply have them where they want them and have no reason to change. But that submission is WASTED because they are not using it in the power of the Holy Spirit to startle the husband for

11

Christ. There are things a wife should SAY to her husband even as she submits to him. And when she does this, in the Spirit, the Lord will use it to squeeze his hard heart. This is woman power, and it is awesome. But what woman can use it unless she knows about it? When a godly woman uses this kind of know-how, the situation will definitely NOT remain the same. The husband will either soften and come to Jesus, or he will harden his heart still more. Things could even reach the place where the marriage might have to be dissolved, but the wife will have given the Holy Spirit the best she has for the winning of her mate.

After a number of interviews with this dear lady, through which you have guided her in the steps a wife can take to reach a stubborn and rebellious husband, the time has come where she feels she can't go on. Now she is in your office talking about divorce. She loves the Lord and she is ready to do His will. So you don't hesitate. You reach into your desk and bring out a copy of **The Compassionate Side of Divorce.** You present it to her. She takes it home and prayerfully seeks to apply the principles to her situation. She goes slowly, refusing to jump to an instant decision. That gives the Holy Spirit time to help her make sure it is God's will she wants and not her own.

Finally she makes her decision and takes it to God for His approval. She feels that a divorce is necessary. In her heart she receives the "green light" from the Holy Spirit. Only then does she file for dissolution of the marriage. You have been God's servant to her all the way. You're ready to stand by her and help her as she takes this difficult step, because you know she is determined to be in the center of God's will. Ah, now you need to be prepared for a visit from her husband. He could come storming into your office, saying . . .

"That book you gave my wife caused her to file for divorce."

Satan loves that kind of a situation. Of course the woman used the principles in reaching her decision. That's what the book is for. But she used them in a godly way. However, her irate husband, who was to blame for the separation in the first place, will be angry with you. He might even demand to know how you dared to give such a book to his wife and call yourself a Christian. You have to be ready for that. But that's not really too bad, you see. The BOOK becomes the real target, not you. That lets you off the hook. So this book is decidedly helpful for the counselor.

OTHERS MAY CRITICISE YOU

The fact that you, a Christian counselor, would even hint that a marriage should be legally dissolved, could earn the scorn of some of the brethren. There are many Christians who sincerely believe the "letter of the Law" should be upheld, and that there are no exceptions. They'll accuse you of letting down the bars and advocating something God hates. Some will probably remind you of the VOWS people make when they get married and divorce amounts to breaking those solemn vows.

Now that's funny. When a Catholic priest, for example, breaks his vow to the Roman church — a vow every bit as solemn and binding as the marriage vow — evangelicals think that's all right. They praise the Lord and tell the ex-priest that he did the right thing in breaking with Romanism. To them it was an evil thing. But when it comes to a husband or wife renouncing the EVIL in a marriage situation, they're not willing to be consistent and apply the same reasoning.

13

What then should your attitude be when criticised by other Christians for trying to help God's people in a hard place? Sympathetic. Nod your head affirmatively when they take you to task. Be gentle with them as you explain your situation:

"Brethren I know God hates divorce, I hate it too. I don't defend it for a minute, for it is rarely the solution. But I also know that God loves the divorcee and accepts him. Yes, He hates divorce, but He doesn't hate people just because they are victims of His program. I do my best, as the Spirit leads me, to help His people when they get caught between those two propositions ... His hatred for divorce and His love for them ... and the best way I know to do that is to employ the toleration principle."

Of course you'll have to explain that last remark.

"Here's a doctor. He's faced with the decision to cut off a man's arm. If he doesn't, the man will die. Certainly no doctor likes to cut off a person's arm, but he will do it rather than have the whole body perish, right? Well God feels the same way. He hates divorce, but He'd rather tolerate a divorce than see a life ruined in a deadly marriage situation. Some marriages are so destructive they can ruin a person's whole life and cripple them spiritually. That means they could suffer from it forever. So what it really boils down to is a question of the lesser evil. When the marriage is WORSE THAN DIVORCE, then divorce is the lesser evil. Certainly God does not insist on the greater evil."

• Divorce is a hard thing for evangelicals to face.

14

Why? These are the very people who long to uphold God's standards. Anyone who loves God's Word feels that way. But, like it or not, divorce is here and we have to face it. Christian marriages are crumbling right and left. To stand behind Scripture verses and condemn these Christians doesn't help anything. We've got to handle it better than that. Yet, the counselor who deals with this problem from the compassionate side, does indeed run the risk of criticism from other Christians. However there does seem to be a softening of hearts in some evangelical circles today.

NO DEFENSE FOR DIVORCE

This book was NOT written to defend divorce. Divorce is an evil. It is the end of the line, the last resort. And the author is the first to admit it. And as a counselor for many years, I know that in most cases, divorce is NOT the answer for those trying to escape from marital pressures. Those who try, find they have merely exchanged one set of trials for another.

Yet this book does advocate divorce — but only when a marriage itself has become dangerous. When a marital union threatens **to destroy** the very people it was meant to build, then it does indeed become WORSE than divorce. This book was written to help believers determine when that time has arrived and weigh their decisions before the Lord. But as for justifying divorce, that is NOT its intention. Also, the book was written to bring relief to those who are **already casualties** of the marriage program. The intention is that it will salvage those lives for Christ. When these people learn the toleration principle and discover how God feels about them, they are set free from the satanic notion that God is through with them. For these people, the book is a miracle.

15

• Here's a Christian who is divorced, but loves Jesus with all his heart. As a counselor, it should be a thrill to put this book into his hands. Let him learn the toleration principle and watch the effect on his life. Why — it's almost magical! Sure, there will be many who can't understand how these people can suddenly come to life, but God is in the resurrection business. When you see these people back in fellowship with Jesus, God's mercy shines in its majestic glory!

So, dear counselor, prize the wonderful tool that has come into your hands. Use it wisely and you will become God's instrument of mercy to a lot of people who need His help. Even if you must bare the criticism of those dear brethren who don't understand the mercy of God, it will be worth it when you stand before Jesus in that day and hear His, "Well Done!" Then you'll say to yourself . . .

"I'm glad I was a compassionate counselor!"

Chapter One

MARRIAGE — A WEDDING OF HEARTS

"For this cause shall a man leave his father and mother and cleave to his wife, and they twain shall become one flesh . . . wherefore they are no more twain, but one flesh. What therefore God hath joined together, let not man put asunder. They say unto Him, 'Why did Moses then command to give a writing of divorcement, and to put her away?' He saith unto them, 'Moses because of the hardness of your hearts suffered you to put away your wives; but from the beginning it was not so.' " (Matt. 19:5-8).

In the beginning it was not so.

It was a glorious moment when the first man stepped forth from the hand of God in response to

17

the divine statement, "Let us make man in our image and in our likeness," but at once we see that it was also an unfinished situation. Behold Adam standing in an elevated place - with the animals, in pairs, passing before him in review.

CREATION OF ADAM
What a glorious moment when the first man
stepped forth from the hand of God!

The Scripture tells us that God brought every living creature to Adam to see what he would call them

— a thrilling sight, perhaps, but also a lonely one. The same chapter of Genesis testifies sorrowfully, "And there was not found a helper for Adam." The Lord God said, "It is not good that the man should be alone." How true it was! The cow could call and its mate would answer back, the lion could roar and a roar would be returned, but all that Adam got back was the echo of his own voice. It was obvious. Man simply was not made to be alone. Certainly though, if he were to have a mate, she could not come from the lower animals.

CREATION OF EVE

God did a marvelous thing. He caused a deep sleep to come upon Adam. From one of his ribs, he brought forth Eve.

Then God did a marvelous thing. He said, "I will make a helper for Adam," and He caused a deep sleep to come upon him. From one of his ribs, He brought forth Eve. When God presented the woman to the first man he exclaimed, "Ah, this is now bone of my bone, and flesh of my flesh — this is my own." Adam need be lonely no more for the blessed marriage program was born.

Adam and Eve started the ball rolling. The first pair took each other to heart and were solemnly joined by God Himself. There was no preacher present to solemnize the event; no rings were exchanged and no vows taken. What really occurred was a **joining of hearts** — a wedding of hearts in the presence of God. This is what God intends marriage to be and what the expression, "married in the sight of God" really means. The union that God witnessed and blessed in the garden is that which He seeks in marriage partners today. His concept of marriage has not changed even though the fall of man brought in corruption and made the salvation program necessary.

GOD'S PURPOSE IN MARRIAGE

A heart-warming truth of marriage comes to mind when I ask the question, "Why did God make man? What was His purpose in making man in the first place?" Surely God wasn't out of work when He made man; it wasn't because He didn't have anything else to do. No, God actually **needed** man, so that in making us He made us for Himself — for His own personal requirement.

20

The Bible declares that God is love. But if He's a God of love, as we all agree, then He needs someone to love. There is no point in being a God of love and a lover **unless** there is someone to love. Just as none of the lower animals could satisfy Adam, so can nothing less than God's own image satisfy Him. As it took Eve to meet the need of Adam's heart, so also does it take man to meet the need of God's heart. Thus it was that He made man in His own image that He might love him and be loved in return. We could say in romantic language — if we dare — that God and man were "made for each other." A flip expression perhaps, but one which highlights the truth of God and man.

Man is not only made in the image of a Lover, but also of a Giver — The Great Giver. The future fellowship that God has planned for His people is one where the climate is total self-giving. No one will live for himself there; only for Christ and for others. Thus it is that the great plan of God calls for man to spend a probationary time upon the earth where he can learn **by experience** how to give himself to another — how to be gentle and kind, long-suffering and forgiving. Only through the experiences of life here on earth can one acquire these graces of godliness.

If this life is the training ground and preparation for the life to come, then marriage must fit into this scheme. How this might be is not difficult to discover. There is no part of life which is not touched by marriage in some way. In fact, marriage is the great center of earthly life as we know it. If it is so central to life, then it must also be central to God's training program. Thus marriage becomes the great laboratory where man learns supreme lessons in self-giving. When a husband and wife truly learn to give themselves to each other, are they not then being prepared for heaven where SELF-GIVING IS THE GRAND THEME?

The major function of marriage is to provide us with the opportunity to grow in Christlikeness, with the reproduction of children as a by-product.

We find then, that the end of marriage is to provide us with the opportunity to grow in Christlikeness. This is the major function, with the reproduction of children a by-product. **Now** marriage takes on a new look. If this life is one of **stresses** calculated to produce Christlikeness, then marriage is at once the center of this stress. To be a place of growth, marriage must also be a place of stress. Man does not grow apart from stresses. Therefore marriages that are successful in the eyes of God, are those where the couples continue to gain victory over their struggles and mature in the process.

Often it is thought that marriage is something of a utopia where couples float through life on a sea of bliss.

Often it is thought that marriage is something of a utopia where couples float through life on a sea of bliss. Teenagers frequently dream of marriage in this fashion and picture it as a romantic journey through life on "cloud nine." Indeed, it can be said of those marriages where the couples report they have no arguments or dissatisfactions with their mates, the purpose of God in their marriage is defeated. Civilizations that experience too much ease fall apart from within, and the same disaster often overtakes those marriages which are completely without stress. God intends marriage to be stressful (not distressful), for it cannot accomplish His purpose otherwise.

Marriage is stressful by **design.** When we consider the marriage law itself, we see that it cannot be any other way. Here is a holy law that takes two people from different backgrounds and environments, cultures, likes and dislikes, passions, appetites, circumstances, intellectual levels and religious differences often, and forces them to live together under the same roof till **death do them part** — as one person! Such a situation is bound to be stressful; in fact, it is something of a miracle when it **is** done. For two people in this setting to overcome their differences and give themselves to each other takes miracle-working power.

BUT WHAT IS MARRIAGE ITSELF?

If it takes supernatural power for marriages to succeed as God counts success, then it is easy to see why so many persons experience difficulty at the center of all living. The only miracle worker we know is the Lord. Thus no marriage can genuinely succeed unless God is party to it. To be sure, many people manage to **exist** under the same roof in a state of matrimony. Their cohabitation is socially acceptable inasmuch as a wedding certificate hangs on the wall. They have their usual share of squabbles, raise their children, and somehow manage to get through life without having to change partners in the middle of the course. Those about them are satisfied that their marriage is normal, but oh how different this is from what God has in mind. Surely His plans for Adam and Eve included more than that.

Marriages appearing as "social successes" which seemingly conform to the standards of society, are a present necessity. But one has to be careful not to confuse this practice with God's view of marriage. Fallen man and God do not see

24

eye to eye on marriage at all. Man is very happy if he can get a preacher to utter some religious sounding words while he and his female companion hold hands. The exchange of rings and the signing of a certificate add to make the transaction more binding and "official." Of course, God is unimpressed with the whole business unless He, Himself, is involved. Not that He isn't sympathetic - He is always interested and sympathetic to the affairs of men, but it must grieve Him some to have a carnal procedure labeled, "holy matrimony."

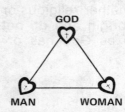
GOD

MAN   WOMAN

Holy matrimony is a trinity. The man, his wife and God in an alliance that witnesses the three giving themselves to each other. Two people may be joined in a social and legal fashion and indeed it is matrimony, but it is not **holy** matrimony without the **Holy One.** The miracle of marriage can never be accomplished without the Miracle Worker's power, and as a result legally joined people often continue to live together in a marriage after the flesh. These people feel an enormous responsibility to stay together too, so that long after their hearts have been separated, they will continue to live under the same roof.

It is when God brings two lives together **unto Himself** and arranges for their full heart dedication to each other, that it can be said, "What God hath joined . . ." Civil and church ceremonies, with all their form and careful words, cannot effect holy matrimony. God does that even as He did in the Garden. At best man can only recognize "what God hath wrought."

SUMMARY

Marriage is an earthly program which brings two

people together for the specific purpose of teaching them how to give themselves to each other. This is in preparation for the **self-giving** fellowship of heaven. As the central institution of earthly life, marriage forms a giant laboratory to produce God's own likeness in believing Christians by means of the calculated stresses that attend it. Marriage is a union of hearts — not a joining of bodies. It is the complete dedication of two people to each other until death separates them, and may be referred to as "holy matrimony" **only** when the Holy One is involved as a third partner. Ceremonies and customs surrounding the modern marriage situation, whether religious or otherwise, are of purely human origin and do not effect the character of marriage as God has ordained it.

Chapter Two

DIVORCE AND THE LAW

"For I hate divorce, says the Lord . . ." (Mal. 2:16 RSV) "And they said, 'Moses suffered to write a bill of divorcement, and to put her away.' " And Jesus answered and said unto them, "For the hardness of your heart he wrote this precept. But from the beginning of the creation God made them male and female" (Mark 10:4-6).

THE MARRIAGE LAW — PERFECT AND ABSOLUTE

If the word of God is emphatic with respect to marriage, it is even more so in the matter of divorce. Here we reach ground that has embarrassed the church for centuries. By virtue of its office and function, the church must uphold the Law of God without compromise. The Scripture is clear — God hates divorce and His marriage law does not provide for it. For God to announce a divine law and later on grant exceptions to it, would suggest that His laws were imperfect and need corrections to care for early oversights.

No conservative Christian is willing to admit that God's Law needs changing or that it is possible for God to err in its early establishment. The orthodox believer insists that God is perfect and that His laws, which are a reflection of His own perfection, are perfect too. He insists with David, "The Law is perfect, reviving the soul . . . ," and avows that when God says, "Let not man put asunder," He means just that. No room is granted for exceptions of any kind.

Jesus' words, which seem to permit divorce under a certain unique circumstance, really do not do so at all when examined in the light of their day. Jesus, as God in the flesh, could scarcely be found authoring a divorce law to amend the original statute. These passages, treated separately in another chapter do not teach divorce as we think of it today, but have a peculiar reference to the ceremonial customs of New Testament days. (See chapter four.) Were it otherwise, God would be **correcting Himself.** If divorce is to fit into the divine scheme at all, it must come as a means of **fulfilling** the Law, not as an amendment to it.

JESUS UPHELD THE ABSOLUTE NATURE OF THE MARRIAGE LAW

Jesus made it quite clear that He had come to "fulfill" the Law, not to change it or correct it at any point, and the Pharisees learned this when they sought to trap Him with legal questions. They asked, "Is it lawful for one to divorce his wife for every cause?" (Matt. 19:3). They were well aware of what Moses had been forced to do when it was determined that the marriage law could not be strictly enforced. Now they would see what Jesus would say about the matter. As the true prophet of God and the clearest expositor of the Law, He recited for them the original statute. "Have ye not read," He asked, "that He which made them at the beginning made them male and female . . . wherefore they are no more twain, but one flesh? What therefore God hath joined together, let not man put asunder" (Matt. 19:3-6). As the true and accurate commentator of the Law He could do nothing other than uphold the perfect standard.

BUT WHAT ABOUT MOSES?

The Pharisees suspected that Jesus would reply with the absolute standard, for He had already declared that not one jot or tittle would pass from the Law until all was fulfilled (Matt. 5:18). They were ready for Him and immediately brought up Moses' situation in the wilderness. "Why did Moses then command to give a writing of divorcement and to put her away," they asked? (Matt. 19:7). They were delighted to raise this matter, and perhaps secretly hoped that Jesus would respond with the perfect marriage law so that they could pin Him down with the wilderness divorce situation. As far as they were concerned, Moses' action constituted a part of the divine Law and they thought it would be very interesting to see how Jesus would reconcile Moses' word with the original statute.

DIVORCE IN JESUS' DAY

The religious leaders of the Jewish nation were

29

delighted with the Mosaic tradition that had been handed down to them from preceding generations. With each succeeding handling it had become more and more corrupt, so that by Jesus' day divorce was considered very nice as long as it was accompanied by the proper bill of writing. Divorce had become more prevalent than in the days of the prophets.

The scene with Jesus and the woman at the well affords a fine commentary on divorce in that time.

The scene with Jesus and the woman at the well affords a fine commentary on divorce in that time, "For thou has had five husbands, and he whom thou now hast, is not thy husband . . ." (John 4:18). This was not an exceptional case, but a genuine symptom of the disease that had infected all Israel. Rome, who dominated Israel, was seriously infected too; even to the place where women boasted of the numbers of their husbands and collected rings upon their fingers in evidence of their pilgrimage of sin.

It was true that Moses had instituted divorce procedure in the wilderness and the statute is clear:

> **"When a man hath taken a wife, and married her, and it come to pass that she find no favor in his eyes, because he hath found some uncleanness in her: then let him write her a bill of divorcement, and give it in her hand, and send her out of his house. And when she is departed out of his house, she may go and be another man's wife"** (Deut. 24:1,2).

The Pharisees were glad for this record. They called it the Law of Moses and delighted in the license they took from it. All sorts of abuses stemmed as a result, to the place where one leading school of theology (Hillel) taught that a man might put away his wife for **any** cause. A book of the Apocrypha supported it: "The Son of Sirach saith, If she not go as thou wouldst have her, cut her off from thy flesh, give her a bill of divorce and let her go" (Ecclus. 25:26). Josephus, the Jewish historian, wrote of himself that he had put away his wife after she had borne him three children.

 This was a time when the letter of the Law (they called it a law) gave man license to please his flesh. It is not hard to see how they would seek to exploit Moses' words here, for by shutting their eyes to the **real intention,** they were free to have as many wives as they could manage to care for. They were not interested in the **justice** of the wilderness divorce

program; they sought only to enjoy the liberties they could press from it. They made a great parade of the fact that they kept the Law of Moses and much ceremony and carefulness attended the preparing of the bill. Their interest centered not in the WHY of any divorce, but in the FORM of the bill itself. It had to be drawn up on parchment of a stated size and had to be written in **twelve lines,** neither more nor less. How typical of those who strain at gnats and swallow camels.

BUT WHAT ABOUT MOSES?

The Pharisees were surely laughing within themselves when they put the question to Jesus, for not only was divorce popular among the religious leaders and the people, but the authority for it was the very one by whom came the Law. To them, Moses was the Lawgiver, and he had found it necessary to establish a divorce procedure in spite of the Law's lofty tenets. Now what would this Commentator from Galilee do when confronted with the wisdom of God's ancient prophet?

Jesus replied once again and this time brought them to consider the very thing they didn't want to face — WHY Moses permitted the divorce practice in the first place. It was something that Moses had permitted (suffered), "Because of the hardness of your hearts," He said, "but FROM the BEGINNING it was not so" (Matt. 19:8). Naturally, they weren't the least bit interested in why the practice had become necessary, only in how they could profit from it. Interesting isn't it, that Jesus did not say, "Because of the hardness of THEIR hearts," but YOUR hearts. It was the same type of heart that had occasioned the divorce statute in Moses' day.

32

 Some helpful insight is gained when the background of the divorce bill is considered. In the earliest days of civilization, women were regarded as cattle. The situation was slightly different in Israel, for the founding fathers had been men of God. Yet interestingly enough, Abraham and his grandson Jacob, had a number of wives and concubines. Polygamy was the standard practice among all the nations, though it might be suspected the patriarchs knew better.

When God gathered His people before Him at Mount Sinai, He gave them His Law, and it called for monogamy.

When God called His people out of Egypt and gathered them before Him at Mt. Sinai, He gave them His Law and entered into a covenant with them to make them His personal nation. This one nation was to live among all the others and be an example to them as representative of the one true God. When Israel moved up to this higher plane and was called upon to demonstrate the Law (holiness) of God, marriage was suddenly given its proper place. The HOLY LAW called for monogamy. The revealed pattern was one man and one woman for life — a situation which we have already noted to be impossible apart from the power of God. The new high standard was set and Israel commissioned to live it before the nations of the world.

No sooner was the Law given and the standard set than it was broken. The marriage law, along with others, was almost immediately violated. Not everybody could live with just a certain woman, and when they were compelled to by law, some dreadful things began to occur. The women were abused, kicked out of the homes, and even murdered. The situation became intolerable and something had to be done to prevent the terrible crimes that were occurring. The nation itself would have fallen apart at the seams had nothing been done to relieve the situation.

 It was at this point that Moses was divinely directed to **allow** divorce for the **prevention of far worse crimes.** This was not a moral law that Moses established, but a **concession** granted for the good of the state. It was found better to tolerate divorce, of which God disapproved, than to produce **greater evils** through an enforcement of the marriage law. It actually became an escape valve which prevented

the whole nation from blowing up. Thus, the divorce machinery was a **toleration** of man's inability to meet the divine requirement and at the same time a means of preserving justice.

If the United States passed a law forbidding all divorce and demanded that people continue together regardless of any circumstances, there would be dead wives from one end of the country to the other.

The situation might be better pictured if we imagined the sudden passing of a law which forbade all divorce in the United States and demanded that people continue to dwell together regardless of any circumstance. Why, there would be dead wives from one end of the land to the other. People would fear to marry and would prefer to live together without the legal bond. The situation is bad enough even with the "escape valve" of divorce, let alone thinking of sealing it shut. The number of murdered wives in America is already pretty high. Only the Lord knows what it would be if an attempt were made to enforce the marriage law today.

Because of the abusive and criminal results that followed the attempt at higher living, the Mosaic statute provided that if a man found something repulsive in his wife, he was permitted to divorce her. It didn't have to be adultery or a similar uncleanness, she could be **stoned** for that and her husband would be rid of her in short order (Deut. 22:21, 22). The bill had to do with matters **other than** fornication and adultery and allowed a man to divorce his wife whenever he found things in her which made him **hate her.** It was **hatred** that produced the crimes.

The divorce ceremony brought marriage to an end. The woman could never return to her former husband; this was forbidden. The bill itself was legally drawn up and witnessed to make it a solemn and final transaction. Actually, it was as solemn as the marriage ceremony which brought the pair together. In all probability, both the marriages and divorces were solemnized by the priests, for Israel was a priestly nation.

The bill of writing was for the woman's protection. If she were cast from the house with nothing in her hand, another man would fear to

36

take her to wife, lest he be charged with living with another man's wife. With nothing to show that she were freed from her former husband, the situation of the woman would be intolerable. The only course open to her, in such a case, was the life of a street walker. A woman found it almost impossible to survive any other way in those times.

BECAUSE OF MAN'S HEART CONDITION GOD EMPLOYS A PRINCIPLE

The story of the ancient nation provides a giant visual aid. The people of Israel demonstrate the difficulty of imposing a high standard upon imperfect men. These were God's own people; He had chosen them "above all the peoples of the earth" and they bore His Name; yet His holy Law ran into serious difficulty when it was imposed upon them. There was nothing wrong with the Law, it was perfect and still is. The trouble lies **not** in the Law, but in the fact that fallen man just cannot keep the Law. "By the works of the Law there shall no flesh be justified," not because the Law is a failure, but because man under the Law is a complete failure. When a perfect law rests upon imperfect men who cannot keep it, something must give way. Thus we are ready to meet a great principle which God employs in dealing with sinful men who cannot even come close to the Law's requirements:

GOD IS WILLING TO **TOLERATE** AN EVIL
WHICH KEEPS HIS LAW FROM
PRODUCING A GREATER EVIL.

The word to notice is tolerate. One of God's great characteristics is His tolerance. He will suffer long with man and tolerate a great deal, because He loves so much. He is far more tolerant than we. Though He

37

is perfect and has every right to be critical and judgmental, He is not. Instead, He tolerates men. Isn't it strange how we are so intolerant of others, yet we want God to tolerate us. We would like to have Him bring the full force of the Law down upon the heads of others for their evil deeds, but we expect mercy when He deals with us.

THIS PRINCIPLE IS IN KEEPING WITH THE SPIRIT OF THE LAW

While the high and holy Law of God may not be compromised because it represents God's own nature, His dealing with man **under that Law** is a different matter. It is also a part of God's nature to forgive and do what He can in mercy to bring man into fellowship with Himself. He is not a Lawyer. He is a Father. He is just in all of His ways, but the ends of justice are not always served by handing out punishments. Sometimes justice is better served by extending mercy to lawbreakers. Frequently a merciful dealing can bring lives closer to the Law's demands than punishment.

Punishment is a vengeful process, and our God will employ mercy and kindness when it can bring men close to Him. Naturally, it takes a very understanding soul to work with men in such a fashion, but our God is that great. Thus, if a greater good can be accomplished by **setting aside the letter** of a statute, God is willing to do it.

None of God's rules or laws are given for their own sake. They have a purpose, a goal, an end. The Law itself is a means to an end, for the end of the Law is not LAWKEEPING . . . but CHRIST-LIKENESS. This is why Christ "is the end of the Law for righteousness to every one that believeth" (Rom. 10:4). The Law was given to reveal the holiness of

38

God so that men could know what He is like and seek to be like Him. It was not given to kill them. True, it does reveal men as sinners and far from what God desires in them, but it would be doing the highest job if it could bring men to godliness. It couldn't do this and that is why Christ had to come.

When God gave the Law to man it was not meant to be his executioner, but his friend and guidebook, so that of his own free will he could grow toward the likeness he beheld there. The Law was made for man, man was not made for the Law. When God finds His own Law working to the hurt of His people, He does something about it. He doesn't bring down the axe. Instead, He tolerantly allows the **letter** to be set aside so that He can accomplish His **real purpose** in a different way. He accepts men as they are — sinners. Even though men are born again through an experience with Christ, they are still sinners. Saved sinners, yes, but still sinners and God deals with them as such.

The very intention of the Law is destroyed when it works to man's hurt. When this happens operational changes have to be made. Because of man's weakness, that which is good can become a dreadful monster. God is willing to make changes to prevent this, yet it is not because the Law isn't perfect, but because it rests on imperfect men. This is Paul's principle thesis when he discusses the Law. He finds the letter to be a killer, ". . . the letter killeth, but the spirit (of the Law) giveth life" (2 Cor. 3:6).

It needs to be noted also that the Law is **spiritual,** not literal. The letter of the Law is a truck that carries the real message of the Law. It is the load inside the truck that is vital. When the letter of the Law is emphasized, it is like placing more value on the vehicle than on its contents. Though the letter of the Law (truck) may be beautiful, it is the spirit (contents) that God is bringing to man. When Paul says, "We know that the Law is spiritual . . ." (Rom. 7:14), he is taking a lot for granted. Not all Christians are aware of this at all. Some obviously prefer the letter and not the spirit, thinking perhaps it is easier to live with the exact situation spelled out in detail. But this not always so.

Take the matter of telling the truth, for instance. The letter demands that one must always tell the truth; never once should a person lie under any circumstances, but the spirit of the Law does not always agree with this. Suppose, for example, you were standing before your house and a terrified young girl, with horror written over her face, brushes past you and runs into your house. In the next moment a frenzied, half-crazed man appears on the scene brandishing an axe. He screams at you, "Did you see a girl go by here? If I can get my hands on her I'll kill her." What would you say? You could tell the truth and reveal her whereabouts, which would mean her life; or you could say, "Yes, I saw her. She went down the street." The lie would save her life. Which would you choose?

Lying isn't nice, but murder is worse. The preventing of the worse evil is more consistent with divine action. The story of Rahab's lie to save the Israelite spies, furnishes a scriptural incident. She sent the agents of the king of Jericho on a "wild goose chase" with her lie, while she hid the Israelites in her home (Joshua 2). For that lie of faith she is listed with the heroes in the book of Hebrews (Heb. 11:31). We might say she lied for the glory of God and was honored because of it. Here the lie fulfilled the spirit of the Law, where the letter could not. Had

Rahab told the truth, none of us would ever have heard her name. She would have perished with the Canaanites.

There is an interesting event in the life of the prophet Samuel that also illustrates the truth of this principle. Samuel, you recall, judged in the days when Saul was king over Israel. God had rejected Saul as king because of his disobedience, and the Lord had informed Samuel of His plans to replace Saul. He then instructed Samuel to go to Bethlehem and anoint one of the sons of Jesse as king, even while Saul was still in power. Samuel protested, saying that he didn't dare do such a thing, for if Saul got wind of it he would slay him.

Then God **Himself** suggested a strategy to Samuel, a means whereby it could be done. It was a subtlety, but necessary because of human nature. The Lord told Samuel to take along a heifer, and if anyone should ask as to his mission, say that he was going to sacrifice. He would thus avoid having to reveal the true nature of his trip. It worked too, for when he reached the town of Bethlehem, the elders asked the purpose of his visit. They feared any trouble and were satisfied when Samuel asked them to join in the sacrifice. Had the prophet been fully truthful in the matter, it would probably have meant his death and caused a revolution in Israel. As unpleasant as using the subterfuge may have been, it prevented the greater harm and accomplished God's purpose (1 Sam. 16:1-13). Remember: It was **God's** idea.

JESUS WAS FULLY AWARE OF THIS TYPE OF DEALING

Our Lord was well aware of the necessity of dealing with man at the human level. The Master

Teacher, who came not only to fulfill the Law in His person and work, but also to expose it in its fullness, completely recognized the weakness of imposing the holy Law upon sinful flesh. He knew also that God subordinated the letter to the spirit, and that sometimes the strict enforcement of the letter could absolutely destroy the very thing that God sought to do; that the letter frequently militated **against** the spirit of the Law. He said as much when challenged over His disciples picking corn on the Sabbath day, "The Sabbath was made for man, and not man for the Sabbath" (Mk. 2:23-28). This was a shock to the Pharisees, who didn't see how anyone could break the letter of the Law and survive judgment. They had no idea as to how God really dealt with man, yet they were **very religious.**

Jesus' pronouncement that the Sabbath was made for man wasn't the end of the matter. He went on to cite an incident from the life of David to show that God will tolerate the setting aside of divinely ordered statutes, when doing so is consistent with His purpose. He asked the Pharisees to recall how that David and those who followed him, had entered into the temple and had eaten the shewbread to satisfy their hunger. The act clearly violated the letter, for none but the priests were to eat of this bread. To preserve David for his glorious reign was more important to God than the law of preserving the bread ... a law, incidentally, which carried a death penalty.

Jesus not only taught this principle, but demonstrated it frequently in His ministry. Healings on the Sabbath day, touching the bier of the Widow's son at Nain are mentionable, but the outstanding example must be His action toward the woman taken in adultery. The Law was specific at this point. The Pharisees reminded Him of this when they brought the woman to Him; "Now Moses in the Law commanded that such should be stoned, but what sayest thou?" (John 8:5). He seemed to be breaking almost every Law of Moses so far, they were wondering what He would do this time. This woman was taken in the very act.

It is a curious bit of history that His words in the sand dispelled the crowd, but more astonishing are His words when the two stood alone; "Woman, where are those thine accusers . . . hath no man condemned thee?" She replied, "No man, Lord." Here we reach the remarkable climax. The Son of God did not pick up a stone to hurl, which well He might, were He to uphold the letter of the Mosaic code. There was no question as to what the letter demanded. Even if no one else cared to obey the ordinance, surely the Son of God would have to obey it. How could He fulfill the Law and not stone this woman?

 Jesus answered, "Neither do I condemn thee; go and sin no more." The letter was deliberately set aside so that the spirit of the Law might be fulfilled. It was more to the glory of God that this woman could become a useful Christian, than that she should be stoned and destroyed. The Law was not meant to kill, and Jesus' action here was fully consistent with the spirit of the Law. The real goal of God for this woman was better accomplished through mercy than punishment. The letter of the Law would have killed her, but the spirit saved her.

How exciting! The Supreme Fulfiller breaking the letter in order to accomplish the spirit. The Great Example making the letter secondary to the main purpose or goal of God. What liberty this brings to those who understand God's heart.

43

GOD'S OWN GREAT USE OF THIS PRINCIPLE

One of the most astounding Scriptural examples where God does not allow Himself to be bound by the Law's letter is in the matter of **war.** Here is something God hates. He detests killing. His Sixth Commandment specifies, "THOU SHALT NOT KILL." It was He Himself, though, who ordered the children of Israel to smite with the sword all the inhabitants of Canaan. The wickedness and idolatry of the Canaanite nations was very great and their judgment had been waiting a long time when God used the nation of Israel as His arm of judgment. Yet, in so doing He broke the very letter of the Commandment which He gave to his people (1 Sam. 15:3).

The greater good was accomplished by breaking the letter. To have His own personal nation overcome by the wickedness of the Canaanites would have been more tragic. To have the "Light unto the Gentiles" destroyed by corruption, was a far greater evil than setting aside the letter of the statute. What a gigantic example — God Himself actually demonstrating the principle of tolerating the evil of killing (war), rather than enforcing the letter to the hurt of His people. This principle then, is not merely implied by the Word of God, God Himself used it.

THE PRINCIPLE APPLIED TO ISRAEL'S MARRIAGE SITUATION

In Israel, even though the people were raised to the standard of monogamous practice, it produced a greater evil in the threat to the mates. To force the one man for one woman law upon the Israelites, with no provision for failure, produced an intolerable situation. The resulting murder and abuse was a violation of a higher law than that of marriage. When

44

the beautiful and holy Law can make men murderers, haters and adulterers, then it is working for evil. Thus divorce can become a means of preventing terrible injustices and God will tolerate it for the sake of His own justice.

Marriage, while high and holy and may be one of man's highest institutions, does not exist for its own sake. Marriage is specifically designed to accomplish something in men's lives. Little is gained by having two people coexist for the sake of doing so. When the higher goal of God is threatened, then the marriage law may be set aside. Preserving rules for the sake of the rules themselves, has never been a penchant of the Lord. I repeat: He is a Father, and not a Lawyer. Marriage is good and holy, but when it works to defeat God's purpose in man, divorce can become the better part, for it more nearly accomplishes God's will. By the same token, however, if divorce were discovered to produce the greater evil, then it would be outlawed by the same principle.

SUMMARY

God has laid down perfect and flawless laws and the marriage law is one of them. There are no exceptions to any of God's laws, hence divorce cannot be an added provision to care for God's failure to consider man's apparent weaknesses. Jesus, as the perfect exponent of the Law, upheld it completely and reaffirmed its flawless and eternal character. The Pharisees' question of divorce raises the matter of imperfect man living under the perfect standard.

The Lord answered the Pharisees with a restatement of the original statute which makes no provision for divorce. When the Pharisees raised the question of Moses' institution of divorce in the wilderness, the whole issue of God's dealing with sinful man comes to view. It is seen that the perfect Law encounters difficulty when imposed upon sinful man. Instead of helping him, it becomes his executioner. Because of this, God must employ a principle which takes man's failure into account. That principle, GOD IS WILLING TO TOLERATE AN EVIL WHICH KEEPS HIS LAW FROM PRODUCING A GREATER EVIL, is scripturally demonstrated in at least five distinct ways:

1. The case of Rahab the harlot, who by faith lied for the Glory of God.

2. The case of Samuel who employed subterfuge, at God's suggestion, to prevent his own murder and revolution in Israel.

3. The case of Jesus and the disciples picking corn on the Sabbath day in violation of the letter of the Sabbath law. Jesus' answer with David and the shewbread incident which violated the temple law.

4. The case of Jesus refusing to stone the woman taken in adultery. A violation of the letter of the code.

5. The case of war. God Himself ordered the Israelites to slay the Canaanite nations in defiance of His own Commandment, "THOU SHALT NOT KILL."

This principle was invoked to heal the desperate situation which developed in Israel through a strict enforcement of the monogamous marriage law. The law was producing injustices, all worse than divorce itself. God's holy Law thus became the means of producing sin. Hence it was in the interest of justice to tolerate divorce.

One day, when the Lord comes in glory, these laws will be fulfilled by the whole of creation. Until that day, however, it is imposed upon sinful men who cannot keep it. God, in dealing with men under His Law, **suffers** divorce as a means of acknowledging **man's** failure; not as a means of acknowledging the **Law's** failure. The divorce statute was an accommodation to a world of sin. While God is holy, He is not unrealistic. The cross stands as supreme evidence of God's awareness that man is helpless under the Law, and that He is willing to make provision for those who are not able to measure up to its holy demands. The cross itself is the most challenging example of the toleration principle. God willingly tolerated the murder of His Son to keep His own Law from sending us to hell!

The cross itself is the most challenging example of the toleration principle. God willingly tolerated the murder of His Son to keep His own Law from sending us to hell!

Chapter Three

DIVORCE AND THE HEART

Not only must God deal with men as sinners, but men themselves are forced to deal with each other on the same basis. The fall of man and the entrance of sin into the human race has made this necessary. From the beginning men have discovered that they cannot trust each other. Out of this unfortunate condition have come many of the customs and practices present today. We may not like to admit it, but a host of modern ways and habits are actually devices to safeguard against human treachery. We have to protect ourselves from one another, and though we may not like these practices any more than God enjoys tolerating divorce and war, they are necessary.

Civil marriage, as such, has grown out of this need for protection. Gifts are exchanged, contracts signed, oaths and pledges taken, and even God's

Name invoked, because man's word is no good. He is a sinner and a liar and socially binding laws and practices have become expedient. Other modern habits stem from this same malady. People are so suspicious of treachery that **notary publics** must validate signatures; monies have to be placed in **escrows** because the parties are not to be trusted; **deposits** are needed to guarantee that one won't back out of an agreement; **oaths** have to be sworn in order to prosecute a perjurer; all because man is depraved and dishonorable. We have become so used to these elements as part of our social climate that we fail to recognize them as symbols of depravity, yet that is what they are.

The fall of man and the entrance of sin into the human race forces God to deal with men as sinners.

In ancient times, marriages were arranged by the parents and the marital partners had little choice with respect to each other. Sometimes amounts of money were posted to make marriage contracts more appealing. The contracts themselves were made as binding as possible, for all too frequently they were looked upon as opportunities for shrewd business tactics. Naturally, they had to be as binding as possible in order to secure and protect the financial interests that depended upon them. The formal wedding vows and publicly witnessed ceremonies of today are born out of this greedy heritage and remain, in part at least, as safeguards against human treachery.

Civil marriage, as such, has grown out of need for protection. Gifts are exchanged, contracts signed, oaths and pledges taken, because man's word is no good.

This is not to say that the practices are bad, of course they are not. They are good and God looks upon them with favor for they help man walk as he ought to walk. Naturally, God would prefer that men would behave in honor, so that their yea meant yea, and their nay, nay. But when this is not to be, the self-imposed restrictions and customs became acceptable. To God, this is "second best." Unfortunately this is where man lives - in the second best area, for he is still a sinner. It is sad that policemen and magistrates are necessary, but they are, and God's Word authorizes these man-made institutions. They are described by Paul as, "Ministers of God to thee for good" (Ro. 13:1-4). Like God, then, man has to accept and tolerate many not-too-pleasant practices, because he is a sinner and cannot measure up to the divine standard.

 The marriage customs and ceremonies, while they have arisen from a background of expediency and necessity, are nonetheless beautiful and important. The licensing features, the home-binding quality of marital vows, the properly witnessed services with all of their color and religious attention, are still very lovely and occupy a vital place in social living. They are not to be despised, but cherished and made as important to family life as possible. What is significant, however, is that they be viewed in their proper setting. **They are not of divine origin.** At best, marriage customs and ceremonies are **human devices instituted by man for his own sake.**

HUMAN PRACTICES CANNOT BE SUBSTITUTED FOR HEART OBEDIENCE TO GOD

Man is so accustomed to human dealings and

accepting the practices that have evolved down through the centuries that he is tempted to regard them as also acceptable in the sight of God. It is easy to forget that God does not view things in the same way as man. Some practices, which are perfectly acceptable to us, could well be unacceptable to God. Many of the customs, ceremonies and rituals which we regard as necessary, may in reality have little or no meaning in His eyes. Thus, any approach to marriage and divorce could not be scripturally proper unless it is considered from **God's viewpoint.**

Inasmuch as God has the ability to look into the human heart and judge the motive and intent, His vision is not restricted to outward ceremonies and rituals performed by man. He sees them, true; but His estimate of them is conditioned by what He beholds in the hearts of the performers. While man is forced to make conclusions on the basis of outward appearances alone, God can look beyond acts and appearances to view the very thinking that produces them. For this reason, our approach to marriage and divorce deals principally with hearts, rather than ceremonies, rituals and legalities. Thus the important feature now is the difference between what God sees and what man sees.

The Lord spoke of this to Samuel when the prophet was seeking out the successor to King Saul. Samuel beheld a fair-looking man and concluded him to be God's choice, but God said: "Look not on his countenance, or the heighth of his stature; because I have refused him:

> **"For the Lord seeth not as a man seeth: For man looketh on the outward appearance, but the Lord looketh on the heart" (1 Sam. 16:7).**

This counsel to Samuel is more than a verse from the Old Testament; it is a deep and profound principle of

Christian living. Any life that would please God must consider this principle, for there is no way to live pleasingly before God if it is disregarded. The statement implies that **all obedience unto God is from the heart.**

Any acts, services or ceremonies that we would offer to God must first be performed in our hearts. The outward behavior then becomes a manifestation of the heart that yearns to do His will. Paul says this; "But ye have obeyed **from the heart** that form of doctrine which was delivered unto you" (Rom. 6:17). Sometimes the deeds may be present, yet the heart far from the will of God. It is when this dreadful practice is extended to religious ceremonies that it becomes particularly hateful in the sight of God.

It was the false showing of outward ceremony that Jesus denounced in His sermon on the mount.

It was the false showing of outward ceremony that Jesus denounced in His sermon on the mount. The Pharisees gave meticulous care to the letter of the Law and made a great show of religious externals. They lifted themselves high in the sight of the people, so that those living in that day surely assumed them to be God's elect; that is, everyone except Jesus.

The Lord Jesus told the people that unless their righteousness exceeded (surpassed) that of the Scribes and Pharisees, they didn't have the slightest chance of entering heaven (Matt. 5:20). He went on to show how the principle of heart obedience applied to the Pharisees and their treatment of the Law. The Pharisees held that if you didn't kill a man, you were fulfilling the words, "THOU SHALT NOT KILL;" but the Lord said the Commandment went beyond the physical act to include even the anger in one's heart. Whether or not it was outwardly expressed didn't matter (Matt. 5:21,22). Clearer yet is Jesus' reference to adultery. The Pharisees judged the Commandment to be obeyed as long as one refrained from illicit intercourse, yet the True Prophet declared lust within the heart to be the same thing as the physical act, in the sight of God (Matt. 5:28).

If we are to obey God then, it must be from the heart. His whole Law is to be obeyed this way. It is also the manner in which it is broken. If we can break it from the heart, we can obey it from the heart. Certainly the Pharisees had no sight of this principle. If they did, they chose to ignore it when they tried to offer God outward ceremonies in the place of heart obedience. Jesus counseled them to take heed of this principle, "But go ye and learn what this meaneth, 'I will have mercy and not sacrifice' " (Matt. 9:13). What a grand summary of the whole matter.

THE HEART OBEDIENCE PRINCIPLE AND MARRIAGE

The principle of heart obedience has serious implications with respect to marriage. The danger of looking upon a civil and human wedding ceremony, as lovely as it is, as **marriage in the sight of God,** is readily apparent. The marriage ceremony, properly a human device instituted by man for his own sake, cannot be offered to God as fulfillment of His marriage law.

Thus we find two sides to marriage; the social or civil side which man has ordained, and the heart side which God has ordained. While both are vital, to confuse one with the other is a serious though popular error. Social customs, imposed by men through expediency and pleasure can scarcely be interpreted as fulfilling the marriage law, any more than religious ceremonies can be understood as fulfilling the other spiritual requirements. One is always in danger of this mistake until he learns to distinguish between what God sees and what man sees.

Men are willing to declare people married when they have stood before a preacher or justice of the peace and he utters some religious words. From that point on it is right in their eyes that these should dwell together and raise children. Everything appears socially acceptable. But God sees not as man sees and His interest is in their heart relationship. He is concerned that two people have genuinely **united their hearts** before Him. In His eyes they are married only when they make the spiritual decision to give themselves to each other. In man's eyes they are not married until they are **socially** joined, have secured the license in legal fashion, and a proper person has offered his pronouncements.

True marriage is a spiritual union and has its

parallel in the salvation experience. In the split second one makes his decision for Christ, he becomes spiritually joined to the Lord. A union of hearts literally takes place. Regardless of any outward expression that might accompany the event, one is **wedded** to the Lord at the time of salvation. It is a time when the believer takes the Lord unto himself, and the Lord receives the sinner unto Himself. He belongs to the Christian personally, and the new Christian is His, personally. All other gods are forsaken and they cleave wholly to each other. It must be a true heart union, for anything less is not salvation.

The beautiful parallel continues for we find no exceptions to the marriage law any more than in the salvation law. God's thinking and planning do not provide that men should come to Christ in holy union and then be divorced from Him. He has no exceptions to His salvation law. In like manner, He has not made any provisions which would permit spiritually wedded couples to separate their hearts from one another. There can be no exceptions to either law for both are perfect in their inception.

We have already noted that the civil marriage ceremony is at best an outward manifestation of an inward heart union. Unfortuntely it can be a **false** one. Man may look upon a ceremony and conclude that here are two hearts truly wedded before God, but only the Lord can judge their real intent. He alone can tell whether or not real heart dedication exists. Wedding ceremonies are too often interpreted as marriage in the sight of God, when **in truth they are not.** In cases where true dedication is missing, the ceremony becomes a false mask. Alas, how often this is true in the things of God.

Because two people join **hands** before a preacher is no guarantee that they have joined

 **hearts** before God. One is no more married in the sight of God through a religious ceremony, than one is saved by joining a church. The joining of hands with a church does not, in any wise, guarantee that one has joined hearts with Christ. The heart may be far from the Lord and church union a matter of convenience. One is an **external act** and the other is an **internal decision.** It is the internal condition of which God takes note.

THE HEART OBEDIENCE PRINCIPLE AND DIVORCE

When we apply the heart obedience principle to the matter of divorce we make a discovery. Not only are there two sides to marriage, but there are also **two sides to divorce.** If marriage has a ceremonial side and a heart side, so does divorce. If in marriage there is that which God sees and that which man sees, the same is true of divorce as well.

DIVORCE TOLERATED

MAN WIFE

In man's eyes, people are said to be divorced when the judge behind the bench pounds his gavel and declares, "Divorce granted." The opinion of society confirms this action and agrees, "Yes, now they are divorced." With God, however, it is a different story. In His sight, the divorce took place **long before** the parties appeared in court. He declared them divorced the moment the husband or wife put the partner out of his or her heart. In that same instant the "Judge of all the earth," said, "DIVORCE TOLERATED." All that the civil ceremony could amount to, was the **outward manifestation of**

57

the inward disunion. The legal action is merely the outward evidence that a heart-separation has **already occurred.** The warring couple would not be in the divorce court otherwise. People go through a wedding ceremony because their hearts have already been plighted. They enter the divorce court only **after** their hearts have been disjoined.

There are many Christian homes that are spiritually divorced, yet there is no outward manifestation of it.

There are many Christian homes that are spiritually divorced, yet there is no accompanying outward manifestation of it. They have not gone to the divorce court, **but they are still divorced as far as God is concerned.** They say, "I can't get a divorce, because I am a Christian. I don't believe in divorce." What they are really saying is, "I don't believe in

LEGAL and CIVIL divorce." They do believe in divorce all right, because they have allowed themselves to be **spiritually separated** from their mates. They are **already divorced from each other in the sight of God** even though there is no human acknowledgement. If one is really concerned with obeying the Word of God, then it is obedience in the **sight of God** that is important, not that which appears acceptable to the community.

Many people continue to live together long after their hearts have been unjoined. True they are not **legally** divorced, but as far as God's marriage law is concerned they are. Without true heart union, these people are living in a **spiritually adulterous state** in clear violation of the seventh commandment. This is what God sees when hearts are alienated, regardless of any human practices used for cover up. Shocking? Indeed!

It's bound to be a shock when one considers that people living together with unjoined hearts are adulterers, but that's what the Word of God declares. It makes no difference to God whether or not a civil procedure has taken place. His records are not altered with the banging of an earthly judge's gavel. The author knows that when these truths register for the first time the reader will be staggered. It is always a shock when we measure ourselves against the holiness of God's Law. When we come right down to it though, we shouldn't be too surprised. Which of God's Laws have we **not** broken? Why should we be astonished to find ourselves sinners in the marriage area? If it is true that, "There is none that doeth good, no not one," and "all have sinned and come short of the glory of God," and "by the works of the Law there shall no flesh be justified in His sight," can we honestly believe that marriage is an exception? No, man is a failure here as well as before any other part of the holy Law.

THE PRINCIPLE OF JAMES 2:10

This logic brings us to another principle God uses in dealing with men under the Law. Again it is expressed in one of those verses which constitute a whole principle in the workings of God:

"Whosoever shall keep the whole Law, and yet offend in ONE POINT, is guilty of all" (James 2:10).

The principle of James 2:10 finds all guilty of God's **whole** law, for all are violators at some point.

For some reason people are ready to condemn those who are casualties of the marriage program. They are barred from church offices, if not from church membership. Frequently they are refused pastoral courtesies simply because they carry the **social** stigma of divorce. It can be nothing more than social stigma — certainly it is not divine disapproval they bear, for that would make God a respecter of persons. Many Christians condemning others through their firm stand against divorce, are themselves divorced in the **sight of God.** Even if they are not legally divorced, they still can't claim to have fulfilled the commandment.

Can anyone reading these lines keep the first commandment? No. It demands that we love God 60 seconds out of each minute so that all of our hours are taken up with living for Him. It demands that we eat, sleep, talk, and behold nothing else but Christ in all our life. Every imagination would envision only Him and every thought and deed would be captive unto Him and performed heartily for His sake alone. Who can claim such personal righteousness? The world has not seen such a man since Jesus.

Who has not been baffled by Jesus' admonition "Be ye perfect even as your Father in heaven is perfect?" Who can do that? "Love your neighbor as yourself," is another challenge that exposes the fruitlessness of any claim to measure up to the Law. Who is there who has not at some time entertained lust within his heart? To all these things we must answer, "Guilty Lord, have mercy upon me a sinner." Yes, we're all guilty before the Law, **even now,** but justified by **faith** in Christ. Praise the Lord!

If this be so, and we judge ourselves failures before **all** the Law, why then, are we so prone to judge and condemn those who stumble over the **letter** of the marriage law? Is that not proof in itself that we behave as sinners, and not as those who have been forgiven every indictment of the Law? When we see ourselves as violators of the Law at every point, the seventh commandment included, we are not so ready to pronounce judgment on others. It may be true that another's sin is out in the open where all can see it, while ours is cloaked by the flesh where only God can see it. How false it would be to accuse, "Ah ha, you dirty dog, run around with another man's wife will you?" while the same evil lurked within our own heart? Yes, fallen man likes to invoke the letter of the Law in judging and condemning others, but he prefers to stand before the cross when viewing his own failures.

61

God is more tolerant and forgiving than we. Even though He has a perfect right to point the finger of scorn, He extends forgiveness instead. Oh, that we could see ourselves as the recipients of His grace and cease to indict others because their failures are of a more public nature than our own.

LET NOT MAN PUT ASUNDER

The principle of heart obedience helps our understanding of certain of Jesus' words. When He says, "What God hath joined together, let not man put asunder," He is not speaking of divorce court proceedings. "Let not man put asunder;" what man? Who? He is not referring to the lawyer who prepares the paper work, nor to the judge who says "divorce granted;" not to the preacher, counselor, or friend, who advises a legal divorce. It can be none of these, now that we have discovered the heart-obedience principle. He is referring to anyone who causes a **separation of heart** between a man and his wife. Such a thing might come as the result of **gossip,** or even the stealing of a partner's affection, The latter bears the legal title, "alienation of affection." God's injunction is directed toward anyone who would cause "heart trouble" in a marriage. In-laws, in particular, should ponder the implications at this point.

SUMMARY

The theological term describing man's plight, as a result of the fall and the entrance of sin into the world, is "total depravity." This means that man, because of his sinful nature, is unable to measure up to the divine standard. The introduction of the sacred commandments revealed man's terrible condition — he could not keep the Law at any point. God, in accepting sinners, finds it necessary to tolerate some of man's sinful practices. Otherwise He could never invite men to come as they are.

Sinners dwelling with sinners find that they too must accept certain practices as necessary safeguards against the treacherous fallen nature. The marriage ceremony, even as it is known today, has its origin among these safeguards. In its best sense it is purely a human device instituted by man for his own sake. That this is so is seen in the fact that marriage, in the sight of God, has to do with the inward union of hearts rather than the outward joining of hands in religious display.

Preachers and justices do not marry people. Couples marry each other. When they forsake all others to CLEAVE TO EACH OTHER, the union becomes blessed in the sight of God. Outward ceremonial forms are merely **human** recognition of the marriage that has taken place. It is much the same as when a church ordains a man to acknowledge that God has **already** set him apart for service.

The offering of human rituals and ceremonies to God as obedience to His Law, was the error of the Pharisees. To offer wedding ceremonies to God today, as the fulfillment of His wedding Law, **is the same error.** God's vision is not the same as man's, inasmuch as He beholds the very thinking of the heart. Those that would please Him should know that He counts what He sees in the heart as the real **act.** This is demonstrated in the teaching on heart adultery (Matt. 5:28).

The same principle holds true with respect to divorce. The appearance of two people in the divorce court is outward evidence that a spiritual divorce has **already** occurred. God's word reveals that those who dwell together with **hearts disjoined** are living in a state of spiritual adultery and as violators of the seventh commandment. Whether or not this is acknowledged by means of a legal divorce has no effect on God's record. The heavenly court does not respond to the pounding of a human judge's gavel. Neither, "I pronounce you man and wife," nor, "divorce granted," has the effect of changing things in heaven.

Both marriage and divorce are inward decisions. God's view of them is independent of the outward ceremonies that attend either one. The principle of James 2:10 finds all guilty of God's **whole** Law, for all are violators at some point. To consider one's inner guilt before the Law makes him less likely to condemn those whose faults suffer public exposure.

Chapter Four

JESUS AND PAUL ON DIVORCE

I don't intend to bring a wordy exposition of the New Testament passages that deal with divorce. Instead, I want to show that the "principle" approach, far from working despite to the Word of God, actually honors it. When one can come to the Bible seeking its **INTENTION,** rather than the exactness of its letter, he gains many fresh insights.

JESUS AS THE TRUE TEACHER OF THE LAW

When Jesus deals with the Law, as He does in His famous sermon on the mount, He speaks as the TRUE PROPHET of God. Moses, when giving the Law, declared that one day another Prophet like himself would come and truly teach the Law unto the people (Deut. 18:15). That day arrived when Jesus began to preach and teach the **intention** of the Law to His disciples. A careful examination of His sermon reveals that He was actually taking the message of Moses and, (1) stripping it of the corruptions that were added "by them of old time," and (2) bringing out the meanings God had in mind when first He gave it.

In every case, where Jesus speaks of marriage, He upholds the divine statute and declares the very things God purposed from the beginning. His repeated use of the phrase "In the beginning it was not so," is evidence of this. Never once does Jesus teach divorce; that is, never does He offer men **any escape** from marriage as God ordained it.

 There are four significant Gospel passages dealing with the subject: Matt. 5:27-32; 19:3-12; Mark 10:1-12; Luke 16:18. Interpreters are particularly disturbed by Jesus' words which appear in two of these; "SAVING FOR THE CAUSE OF FORNICATION" (Matt. 5:32; 19:9). These six words can be real trouble makers. If not properly handled, they place Jesus in the position of **changing the Law.** Isn't it unthinkable that the One whose avowed purpose was not to "destroy the Law or the prophets" should suddenly appear and announce a change in the marriage law? It was the Lord's own testimony that the Law of God is eternal, unchangeable and perfect.

Beyond this, the Law itself is a reflection of God's own nature. Since that nature is not subject to change, neither can be the Law. This same Law will one day be fulfilled in Christ's kingdom on earth. Any changes made before that time, based on man's sinful condition, would bring an imperfect Law to the kingdom. Yet, here stands Jesus' annoying excep-

66

BUSINESS REPLY CARD

FIRST CLASS   PERMIT No. 14599   PHILADELPHIA, PA.

POSTAGE WILL BE PAID BY

Eternity

1716 SPRUCE STREET,
PHILADELPHIA, PA., 19103

A Special Offer for "Over-the-Shoulder" Readers:

Mail this card to

Eternity

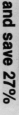
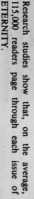

and save 27%

Research studies show that, on the average, 115,000 readers page through each issue of ETERNITY.

But only 60,000 copies of ETERNITY are printed each month. That means 55,000 of you are "over-the-shoulder" readers!!

Why not get your own copy of ETERNITY each month? Save on neck and eye strain. Have ETERNITY on-hand to read when it's convenient for you.

As a subscriber, you qualify for special Savings off the regular single-copy rate.

That means you get the next 11 monthly issues of ETERNITY for only $11.87 (instead of the regular $16.50 single-copy price). Or the next two years for just $21.78 ($11.12 off the regular $33.00 single-copy rate).

tion squarely in the middle of a discussion on marriage. If not carefully handled, it can be made to show that there is a time when the holy Law may be broken by men and **not bring guilt.** If, however, it can be shown that the Lord's exceptive clause does not apply to HEART-MARRIAGE but something else, then Christ is not the author of a divorce law at all.

THE EXCEPTIVE CLAUSE

I have insisted that the Word of God does **not teach** divorce, but merely **tolerates** it. The question may then be asked, "What does Jesus mean when He says, '. . . that whosoever shall put away his wife, SAVING FOR THE CAUSE OF FORNICATION, causeth her to commit adultery . . . ?' " Is He declaring that there is a time when the statute may be set aside? Is He here actually authoring a divorce law? To admit to such a thing would amount to saying that God's laws were not perfect when decreed and in need of later modification.

No, the answer has to be found in some area other than that of the **heart-union** of a man and wife. The exceptive words must not refer to the spiritual marriage union itself, but to some part of the marriage **situation** as it existed in that day. It is when the remark is viewed in **the light of ancient marital practice** that it is revealed how Jesus' words are to be taken.

 It was common for Israelite parents to arrange the marriages of their children in the most tender years; some were known to be pledged before they were born. The Jewish parents often considered the financial and family tie aspects of the match

more important than the heart union. Frequently, the bethrothed couples never saw each other until the day their marriage was consummated. Regardless of whether or not they had laid eyes on one another, they were considered married under the Law and referred to as husband and wife. In the last year or two preceding the consummation, the fact of the marriage received public recognition.

This pre-consummated state of marriage was similar to today's practice of being engaged. The ancient couples were seldom in love as we know engaged people to be. There are many places in the world where this practice still continues. In India, for example, it is quite common.

The fornication that Jesus mentions as an **exception** to the marriage state, refers to the uncleanness or unchasteness that a man might discover in his wife **AFTER** they began to live together. Such a thing amounted to FRAUD in the marriage contract. Why? The husband believed himself to be gaining a virgin of Israel. In this case it would have nothing to do with the putting of a wife **out of one's heart** (spiritual separation). Thus it would not be touching the holy marriage law. The exception is not **legalizing heart disunion,** but terminating a **civil contract.**

The Old Testament provided that when fraud of this nature was discovered in a woman, the husband had every right to cry "foul" and have the woman ceremoniously stoned. If Jesus is providing an exception to any law at all, it would not be the marriage law — but the STONING LAW. **He is saying that under such circumstances let the man put away his**

wife rather than have her killed. At any rate we are certain that the exception does not deal with the divine marriage law, but a feature of marriage CUSTOM instead.

It is reasonable that a man cannot pledge his devotion to a woman and become one flesh with her when it is known that she purposely intended to deceive him. If, as God's Law declares, "For this cause shall a man leave his father and mother and cleave unto his wife; and the twain shall be one flesh . . ." truly deals with the giving of hearts, then such a union could not take place under **fraudulent** circumstances. According to the custom in Israel, heart dedication did not occur until AFTER the marriage consummation, therefore the putting away would have to occur later also.

In Jesus' personal family history this matter was significant. Before Joseph and Mary "came together," Joseph found her to be pregnant.

In Jesus' personal family history this matter was significant. Before Joseph and Mary "came together," as the Scripture says, Joseph found her to be pregnant. He was minded to put her away privately instead of having her stoned, and it was while he was contemplating this action that the angel revealed the scheme of the virgin birth. No doubt Jesus was familiar with this circumstance, as well as with the customs of the day, and His remark was made to **clarify** the fraud idea rather than to bring a specific teaching. It was as if He were saying:

> No man shall ever put away his wife for any reason, except of course when the betrothal itself is a fraud; that is understandable. But when two people give their hearts to each other before God, any disunion of that bond, regardless of the reason, produces an adulterous state.

This, I believe is the intent of Jesus' words.

SUCH AN EXCEPTION TO THE MARRIAGE LAW IS UNNECESSARY

For Jesus to author a divorce law which permitted a man to put away his wife after they had become one flesh, would not only teach a violation of the commandment He had just stated, but would find Him **destroying** the Law. The feature which makes the suggestion even more inadmissable is the fact that such a provision is actually **unnecessary.**

According to Jewish Law, all that a man would have to do in this circumstance would be to complain to the magistrate, and after a confirmation of the charges, the woman would be

70

stoned to death, **eliminating any need for a divorce.** (Deut. 22:13-21). For Jesus to reiterate the holy commandment and then proceed to make an **unnecessary change,** would demonstrate utter disregard for God's Law. No, His statement must be understood as having to do with **betrothal fraud** and not as an exception to divine matrimony itself.

Not all Bible teachers will be happy with this explanation. To some it is too facile. They argue that the context, particularly in Matt. 19:9, demands that the consummated marriage state is in view rather than the betrothal period inasmuch as the discourse begins with a pronouncement of the original statute. Yet it is for this very reason that the writer feels Jesus could not be authoring an exception to God's program. Quite obviously the consummated state is in view, for that **is** the time when the fraud would be discovered, but **true heart-marriage** is not in view. It is Jesus' careful insistence of the original law that certifies He had something other than the breaking of heart-marriage in mind.

This approach becomes more satisfying when it is noted that the context of the entire sermon on the mount (Matt. 19:9 is obviously an excerpt) is righteousness through heart-obedience (Matt. 5:20). The righteousness that God wanted in His people had to come from their hearts rather than the showy and external means used by the Scribes and the Pharisees as they performed the letter of the Law. It would be strange indeed for Jesus in a "heart" sermon to teach in one breath that fornication and adultery occurred in the heart with the **look of lust,** and then in the next breath allow that fornication provided a just and lawful reason for terminating a heart marriage. Such an exception would grant that almost every marriage in the land could rightly be dissolved on the basis that all of us are **heart-adulterers.** If the **exceptive clause applies to true**

marriage, then the Bible **does** teach divorce, and it is obtainable on the easiest and most natural grounds. It all changes when the matter is viewed from the heart, for that is the way God beholds men.

PAUL AND DIVORCE

Strangely enough, Paul never mentions divorce. He takes to himself the astonishing privilege of **speaking against marriage** itself.

In coming to Paul's thinking on the divorce question a surprise awaits the reader. What will the eloquent exponent of Christian liberty do here? How will the man who says, "All things are lawful for me," and "I am persuaded in the Lord Jesus that nothing is unclean of itself," treat this matter? Will he, who has set himself free from the letter of the Law, turn about and place a yoke about the neck of his readers? Will he once again bring into bondage those to whom he has declared the "glorious liberty of the sons of God?"

vs 16 --(For my determined purpose is) that I
may know Him--that I may progressively become
more deeply and intimately acquainted with Him
perceiving and recognizing and understanding
(the wonders of His person) more strongly and
more clearly. And that I may in that same way,
come to know the power outflowing from His
resurrevction (which it exerts over believers);
and that I may xxxkxxxx so share His sufferings
as to be continually transformed (in spirit into
His likeness even) to His death....

Amplified

No, Paul does not do that. Strangely enough, he never once mentions divorce. He doesn't discuss it anyplace. But he does use freedom in a most peculiar way. Paul takes to himself the astonishing privilege of **speaking against marriage itself.** It is not because he fails to understand the beauty and purpose of marriage that he speaks as he does, for he is fully alert to the glory of marriage as his letters testify. He has other reasons pertaining to the times in which his readers lived. Yet, when we carefully note how he cautions people against marriage, as he does the Corinthians, it can be a shock. A single reading of the seventh chapter of First Corinthians, with this thought in mind, will be enough to convince.

"STAY SINGLE" Paul's liberty is found to be one FROM MARRIAGE ITSELF, rather than one of taking liberties IN marriage. Yet even so, at least two references suggest that he doesn't hesitate to extend his freedom to that area too. Again and again the Bible speaks of the blessedness and necessity of marriage, yet Paul unhesitatingly counsels that people will be better off if they can remain free of mates altogether. He avows, in this mentioned chapter at least, that marriage is a trap and a snare for the Christian, and unless a man cannot help himself, he should avoid the marital bond completely. Paul's comments are uttered as though God did not say:

"It is not good that the man should be alone . . ." (Gen. 2:18).

"A virtuous woman is a crown for her husband" (Prov. 12:4).

"Whoso findeth a wife findeth a good thing and obtaineth favor with the Lord" (Prov. 18:22).

Woman was made for man. The Bible clearly establishes marriage as central to the earthly scheme. Yet Paul feels free to speak to the contrary in this seventh chapter of First Corinthians:

> "Art thou loosed from a wife? Seek not a wife." (vs. 27).

> "But if they cannot contain, let them marry; for it is better to marry than burn" (vs. 9).

> "I say to the unmarried and the widows it is good for them to abide even as I (vs. 8).

> "So then, he that giveth in marriage doeth well, but he that giveth (her) not in marriage, doeth better!" (vs. 38).

> "I would that all men were as I myself: ..." (vs. 7).

> "But I would have you without anxiety. He that is unmarried careth for the things of the Lord, how that he may please the Lord. But he that is married careth for the things of the WORLD, how that he may please his wife" (vss. 32,33).

What an amazing use of one's liberty! Paul sets himself against the divine pattern when he teaches that people are better off to leave marriage alone. Of course, Paul had justification for his unique counsel. But what is significant now is that he was obviously using **God's operating principles** to bring this kind of teaching. Paul knew that great tribulation was at hand and the persecutions the Christians were enduring for Christ marked the beginnings of awful trial (vss. 29-30). He felt that the interest of Christ would be better served if the Christians could avoid all worldly entanglements, and marriage, in view of the "present distress," was one of them (vs. 26). Here is freedom at its zenith — daring even to contradict the divine scheme of marriage and the home because of his convictions. Such boldness demonstrates how thoroughly Paul had loosed himself from the letter of the Law.

ROMANS 7:2

"For the woman that hath a husband is bound BY THE LAW to her husband so long as he liveth; but if the husband be dead, she is loosed from the law of her husband. So then, if, while her husband liveth, she be married to another man, she shall be called an adulteress; but if her husband be dead, she is free from THAT LAW, so that she is no more an adulteress, even though she be joined to another man" (Rom. 7:2,3).

People seeking help in a divorce situation are distressed by such verses. Unfortunately, they read into them something that is not present. Paul is **not speaking of divorce** in this passage. His main context is the Law and people under the Law (vs. 1). It is the relationship of individuals to the Law that is being discussed here, and he is saying that even as a woman ACCORDING TO THE MARRIAGE LAW is bound to her husband until he dies, so are people bound to the Law of God until they die. Only death can separate in either case. As death separates a wife from a husband, so does it also separate a man from the Law.

Even within the illustration itself (and that's all this is) it is not a teaching on marriage or divorce. He is talking about **DESERTION** AND **BIGAMY.** The question of divorce is not even hinted or alluded to. Yet sufferers come to this passage and read into it their own problem. Any woman, Paul is saying, who takes off from her husband and joins herself to another man is an adulteress. It is an act of willful desertion. That is all that he is saying — nothing more. Marriage, remember, is not under discussion here — only the Law. There is danger here for those who bring their personal problem and fail to read past the fourth verse. No conclusion should be reached unless it includes the exciting news of verse six. HERE IS A TRULY PAULINE PRINCIPLE. "But now we are delivered from the Law, that being dead wherein we were held; that we should serve in newness of spirit, and not in the oldness of the letter" (Rom. 7:6).

HERE WE MAKE AN OBSERVATION

People plagued with a problem frequently turn to the Bible seeking loopholes in the Law as a means of escape. This is why some writers like to see divorce taught by Jesus in His exceptive clause. It is human and natural to do this, but it does not supply a satisfactory answer. It is far better, in the opinion of the author, to let the Law of God alone to enjoy its flawless perfection, and seek help in the WAY GOD DEALS WITH MEN UNDER HIS PERFECT LAW.

BEYOND ITS GRASP

Rather than make changes in His Law, God makes provision for men unable to meet its lofty requirements — and that provision is **death!** Does it seem surprising that God would provide such a means as the only proper escape from the exacting demands of the legal code? That is exactly what He has done. The cross itself is a provision made for men under the Law. When we come right down to it, what other way is there for sinners to escape a perfect law? Only by receiving the DEATH OF CHRIST **as their own,** do men find freedom. A dead man is beyond the reach of the Law. Thus when the believer "dies" in Christ, the Law cannot touch him. This is why the cross and the "blood of Christ" are precious to the orthodox Christian. The life on the other side of that death is one of liberty — liberty in the Holy Spirit. How much better is this approach than trying to find "escape passages" in the Written Code. This is the foundation upon which Paul builds his case for Christian freedom.

BUT TO PAUL AGAIN

The reason Paul doesn't discuss the divorce issue is because he doesn't have to; "All things were lawful for him." Divorce, legal bills, putting away and the like were of no particular interest to him because he had come to view things as does God — at the heart level. Paul's tremendous messages on marriage, when he does speak on the subject to the Ephesians and the Colossians, clearly indicate this. To him, divorces and separations were merely the outward indications of the inward heart condition and he would favor any action that was taken in the interest of Jesus as long as the rights of others were not harmed.

Putting the letter of the Law behind him Paul declared, "Whatsoever you do in word or deed, do all in the name of the Lord Jesus . . ." (Col. 3:17). As far as he was concerned the believer, being released from wherein he was held, was delivered from the Law (Rom. 7:6). Paul's chief care was that he did not stumble others in the use of his freedom (1 Cor. 8:13). Apart from stumbling others, however, Paul could do anything and say anything he pleased for the glory of Christ. Here we have a man who truly moved according to **God's operating**

77

principles, since he was motivated by love rather than the letter of the Law.

PAUL'S LIBERTY IN MARRIAGE IS ALSO NOTICEABLE IN I CORINTHIANS 7

In verse 10 Paul instructs the wife not to leave her husband, yet in the next verse he allows "BUT IF SHE DEPART, let her remain unmarried . . . or be reconciled to her husband." It is not difficult to see that Paul is more concerned that she not remarry than he is over her departure. Not only would he have those who do separate remain single, but also those who are loosed by death or divorce to remain unjoined to anyone (vs. 27). Yet, says he, if they do marry, they have not sinned (vs. 28). What a way to put it. If you don't marry you do well, but if you do get married, you haven't sinned.

In verse 15 it is noted that Paul isn't teaching or advocating separation, just referring to it; "But if the unbelieving depart, let him depart. The brother or sister IS NOT UNDER BONDAGE IN SUCH CASES." It appears Paul would have the remaining believer make NO effort to stop the departing one. And if that were not enough, he asks the believer to count himself free and to enjoy God's peace in the matter. It doesn't seem to bother him in this verse, that the letter of the Law would regard them as yoked until death. Surely Paul's view is astonishing. It is almost as if he were glad to see the Christian freed of an unsaved partner. Of course he recognizes the possibility that the unbelieving one could be saved should they continue to live together, and he makes mention of it (vs. 16). The big thing in his mind seems to be that while marriage is **good,** freedom for Christian service is **better.** This truth unquestionably lies beneath all he is saying here.

Paul does a strange thing in verse 39 when he reverts to the Law again, but the author would understand that Paul is so dead set against anyone's remarrying once they are free, that he would cite the Law in support of his contention. Without doubt, where a remarriage was clearly in the interest of Jesus, Paul would be the first to give his blessing. The interest of Christ was all that Paul lived for.

SUMMARY

Jesus Christ, appearing on earth as the True Prophet of God, upheld and defended the eternal and unchangeable character of the Law.

Jesus Christ, appearing on earth as the TRUE PROPHET of God, upheld and defended the eternal and unchangeable character of the Law. When He speaks of the marriage law, He reiterates the original statute and makes no provision for divorce whatsoever. It is not allowed that the exceptive clause, SAVING FOR THE CAUSE OF FORNICATION, is a proviso to heart-marriage itself, but instead, has to do with the betrothal or "engagement" custom of that day. We have seen that Jesus could not be instituting a change in the holy Law for the following reasons:

1. The Law itself is a reflection of God's holiness. Since His nature is not subject to change, His Law cannot change either.

2. Jesus would be granting an exception to the statutes which have already been declared perfect, unchangeable and eternal (Matt. 5:18; Psa. 19:7, 8; Rom. 7:12).

3. Such a provision would make Him the **author** of a divorce law. This would have the effect of destroying the Law rather than fulfilling it (Matt. 5:17).

4. The exception is **unnecessary,** because the wife could be stoned for this very reason (Deut. 22:13-19).

5. It is not God's method to **change** His Law because of man's sinful condition, but to **provide** for man under the perfect Law. Ill.: The cross itself is in this category.

6. The perfect Law is for the perfect kingdom. To author exceptions in the Law, because man cannot meet its strict demands, would bring an imperfect law to the kingdom.

7. Jesus' teaching on heart-adultery labels a great host as fornicators. Were His exceptive clause to pertain to heart marriage, multitudes would be granted the right of legal divorce with divine sanction. (Matt. 5:28).

The answer to the divorce problem is not found in Jesus' teachings of the Law, but in His **revelation** of the Father's heart. Since God views men at the heart level, the obedience He seeks is from the heart. It is possible to serve God with the mind, even while serving the law of sin with the flesh (Rom. 7:25). It is folly to attempt to justify divorce by driving wedges between the letters of the Law. God is not really pleased with letter obedience.

This last truth was beautifully dramatized when Jesus spoke to the rich young ruler (Luke 18:18-24). Concerning the letter of the Law, the young man answered, "All these things have I kept from my youth up ..." Theoretically, the letter was fulfilled. Yet he turned away sorrowful. He was not a bit like the Christ that stood before him. His heart yearned after wealth instead of the will of God. Such a life did not violate the letter of the Law, but it violated the heart of God. Thus we can note:

JUST AS IT IS POSSIBLE FOR ONE TO KNOW THE BIBLE AND **NOT KNOW** THE CHRIST OF THE BIBLE, SO IS IT POSSIBLE TO LIVE BY THE BIBLE AND **NOT LIVE** THE CHRIST OF THE BIBLE.

It is possible to live by the Bible and not live the Christ of the Bible.

PAUL

Whenever Paul referred to the marriage law, he too had the original statute in mind. Paul never once taught exceptions or loopholes in God's Law. He declared it to be good and **just** (Rom. 7:12). One does not have to change a just law. Instead of changing the Law, something Paul knew God could never do, he speaks of God's **provision for men under the Law.** That provision is the **death of Christ.** By receiving Christ's death by faith, men are instantly removed from the jurisdiction of the legal code and free to experience a new life of liberty. Instead of strict cautions governing their lives, they are free to follow Christ as best they can. Paul is explicit when he proclaims the Christian's liberation from under the letter of the Law to enjoy freedom in the Holy Spirit (2 Cor. 3:6).

Paul demonstrates a strange use of his freedom. He takes the liberty of counseling the Christians of his day to refrain from marriage if they can, so that they may give themselves completely to Christ (1 Cor. 7). He is not the enemy of marriage, but feels that the **IMPENDING DISTRESS** makes his counsel judicious. He even invokes the Spirit's witness at that point. When he does speak of marriage, however, his language seemingly goes **beyond** the requirements of the letter of the Law, "So ought men to love their wives as their own bodies" (Eph. 5:28). The letter never demanded anything like that.

When one has truly caught the significance of receiving Christ's death he too can say with Paul, "ALL THINGS are lawful for me," observing only that he does not stumble others in the use of this liberty. This is the life of the Spirit, and, ". . . where the Spirit of the Lord is, there is liberty." (2 Cor. 3:17).

Paul refers to marriage in the midst of a discussion of the Law, but then it is only to illustrate a point. In those places he has reference to DESERTION and BIGAMY, not to divorce. Paul does not discuss divorce at all, and certainly he does not teach it. He would **tolerate** it, as does God. He would not hesitate to suggest it in certain cases, but never would he represent divorce as a part of God's marriage program. It is to a completely different area that one must look before the divorce problem is resolved. That is to the area of **GOD'S OPERATING PRINCIPLES.**

Since the Christian is loosed from the bondage of the Law by receiving the death of Christ, he needs a pattern for his new life. He is free to walk as best he can after the Holy Spirit. That walk is greatly aided when he learns the principles by which God governs His own behavior. He is truly liberated when he discovers the ways in which God deals with sinful men in the face of His holy standard — the very principles set forth in these chapters. It is only after one has discovered that God is a Father and not a Lawyer, that his heart can shout,

"HALLELUJAH, WHAT A SAVIOR!"

Chapter Five

GOD'S OPERATING PRINCIPLES — THE HIGHER GROUND OF CHRISTIAN LIVING

OPERATING PRINCIPLES

There are actually two methods of living out obedience before God. One is where the life is controlled by chapters and verses of the Bible. The other where the life is regulated according to divine operating principles. When one discovers the very principles by which God operates, and allows his own life to be governed by them, it can be justly concluded that he has reached higher ground in the venture of faith.

The chapter and verse approach to Christian obedience might be likened to the time an infant spends in his crib. The bars of the crib, while restricting him to a defined area, permit him to play by himself in comparative security. He can reach

out and take hold of them, and as his strength gains, gradually pull himself up. Finally he can stand and almost walk, and his crib days will have played an important part in his development. He cannot remain in that stage indefinitely however. The time comes when he must leave the prison-like enclosure and step out into a life of higher freedom and self-control. For a child to remain permanently in the crib stage is a heart-sickening tragedy. That which is good for a time, eventually becomes a hideous sight from which people turn their eyes.

When one is born again through faith in Christ, he is a spiritual infant.

The same holds true in the Christian experience. When one is first begotten through faith in Christ (born again) he is a spiritual infant. The new life before him is threatening and overwhelming. He does not know how to use his little hands or where to place his little feet in faith. The chapter and verse approach spells things out for him in reassuring detail. He can take hold of specific Scriptural "bars" and they will give him strength. They help greatly in the early choices of the Christian life. If he develops properly he is soon able to stand. Before long he is ready to move into an area of wider freedom. He will shift from the bars (verses) to a knowledge of his Father's way of doing things and is ready to take some responsibility on his own. This is the way men grow to maturity, whether in an earthly family or the divine family.

Life's Problems

Of course, if one cannot govern himself by the light of his Father's knowledge, then he needs to be controlled externally. When men are not able to handle their freedom, then they must forfeit it. We call such people convicts. They are confined to a supervised jail-life, because they cannot take their place in a free society. The Christian too, if he is not able to live under New Testament freedom, must return to confinement. No longer are the bars (verses) a blessing — now they become a bondage. It is sad that many refusing to face the reality of the Christ-life and its freedoms, must remain imprisoned under the letter of the Law. To reach the place where divine operating principles rather than Bible verses, per se, guide one's actions and decisions, is to arrive at a higher level of maturity.

The most fruitful path of Christian living is that which regards the biblical revelation as

a whole. The very purpose of the Bible is to **reveal** the Lord's heart and will, not to legislate holiness, which is an impossibility. Once the SUM of God's Word begins to dawn, a person is in a position to follow after Christ. The principle of CHRISTLIKENESS becomes his pattern, rather than a slavish conformity to rules. The new Christian learns there is a difference between **knowing the Bible** and knowing the **Christ of the Bible.** The mature Christian learns that there is a difference between **living the Bible** and **living the Christ** of the Bible. The two are not the same.

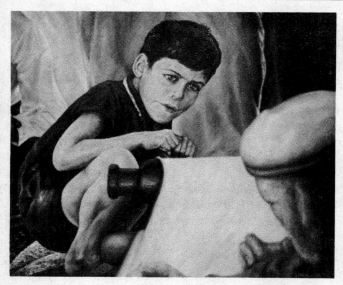

"Did you not know that I was bound to be in my Father's house?"
The life and ministry of Jesus were not guided by isolated passages from the Old Testament, but by His knowledge of the Father's will.

The life and ministry of Jesus were of this order. Surely His steps were not guided by isolated passages from the Old Testament, but by His knowledge of the Father's will. His life outlived that knowledge. True, He was familiar with the ancient Writing, and knew the texts better than the Scribes of His day, but He was obviously **bound by none of them.** The Lord's insight came "precept upon precept" (principle), not only through the instruction He received from His mother and the Sabbath schools, but as He looked to His Father in heaven (Luke 2:52). To Him, the literal rules of the Old Testament were more like tools in a tool box. He chose those which best suited the job at hand. We have already noted how He chose verses of the Old Testament which set forth principles rather than rules (Matt. 9:13; 12:3, 7).

Paul felt free to set aside the old covenant of "THOU SHALT NOT" in favor of, **"WHATSOEVER** ye do, do it heartily as unto the Lord, and not as unto men" (Col. 3:23). The old "ministration of death," as he called the letter of the Law, was all right as a "tutor" to guide man's early steps. But since the fuller revelation had come in the person of Christ, the old legalistic approach was to be abandoned in favor of the new order of Christian freedom (Gal. 3:25). The "glorious liberty of the sons of God" can be enjoyed only when a life is governed by **principles** rather than **CONFORMITY TO RULES** (Col. 2:20-23).

A little child must place his feet on selected rocks in order to cross a stream, but an older and more mature lad may jump or even ford the same brook without danger. His maturity allows him to be free of laboring with each step. The same is true of the new Christian. The letter of the Word helps in guiding his early progress, but its usefulness is **over** when he learns how God thinks and feels and can steer his life by the higher principles. This is not unlike the law of gravity. This good and fixed law is overruled by the higher law of aerodynamics every time an airplane leaves the runway.

Thus, while the "chapter and verse" approach is fine during the period of its usefulness, it is overruled by the adult concept of living by divine principles. Such a way of life neither compromises the holiness of God nor injuries the intent of the Law. Instead it is the very ground of New Testament freedom and maturity. It is the heart of Paul's thinking when he declares the sons of God liberated from the legal bondage of the seventh chapter of Romans, "For the law of the Spirit of life in Christ Jesus has made me free from the Law of sin and death," he says (Rom. 8:2). The freedom he mentions is obtainable only by invoking a higher law or principle. A policeman will rush motorists through a red light in order to make way for an approaching ambulance. The higher purpose overrules the **demand** of the traffic signal. Even highway rules do not exist for their own sake — their main goal is driving safety.

Even highway rules do not exist for their own sake—
their main goal is driving safety.

To keep people under the bondage of rules INDEFINITELY, is to impose a fearful legalism and restrict lives to the letter of the Law. The killing power of this deadly way of living is manifest on the faces of those Christians who are constantly striving to keep rules. They are not happy and their lives show it. Far from enjoying the peace of Christ, they are miserable and their misery reaches out to depress those about them. Many are seriously disturbed to the point of mental and emotional breakdowns, largely because they realize the discrepancies in their own lives. The destructive power of legalism has already been described. Now we see that imposing this dreadful monster on the New Testament is the worst kind of error. It is no more acceptable today than when it received Paul's anathema centuries ago. New Testament legalism is just as hateful as any ascribed to the old order. (Gal. 5:1; 1:8).

To keep people under the bondage of rules INDEFINITELY, is to impose a fearful legalism and restrict lives to the letter of the Law. Many are seriously disturbed to the point of mental and emotional breakdowns.

In offering the reader an escape from rules, the author does not teach any form of lawlessness. The behavior of the Christian must still be **lawful,** for God Himself operates lawfully. The difference is, instead of being bound to biblical rules, he is released to live by biblical principles. He is free to do anything he pleases as long as it does not injure others and is done as unto the Lord (Col. 3:17). The mature believer need not be ashamed of anything he can ask God to bless, regardless of rules to the contrary.

In offering the reader an escape from rules, the author does not teach any form of lawlessness.

Paul must have been thrilled to teach, "Happy is he that condemneth not himself in that thing which he alloweth" (Rom. 14:22). It can be taken without argument that the supreme principle of Christian living is the Law of love, for it is God's own chief motive. All other principles flow from this one.

The New Testament is at its zenith when it reveals Christ in glory; when it unfolds His heart, passion and will. It is a **revelation, not a code.** The purpose of the Written Word is to acquaint men with the Living Word. When they have gained this marvelous insight, they no longer serve the **written details,** but follow the **living person.** There is a difference. When the mature Christian is in doubt as to some matter of life, he turns to the Bible as God's supreme revelation, to learn **what Jesus would do.** He is following a person now. The mature Christian looks past the words of the Bible, that is, the literal wording to discover the heart of the Lord. The question in his mind is, "what would Jesus do?"

The mature Christian looks past the WORDS of the Bible and asks, "What would Jesus do?"

The principle approach is a freedom from **letterness,** but not a freedom from the Word of God. The Bible remains the supreme authority over the Christian's life for it is the **only** revelation of the heart and will of God. When one looks behind the words of the Bible to discover God's heart, he is looking deeper into the Word of God than ever before. In a sense he is, "reading between the lines." More than that, he is grasping the **whole significance** of God's Word to man rather than isolated portions. The principle approach is not extra-biblical, it is **deep-centered biblicism** and represents the finest expression of a Bible-controlled life. For one to reach the higher ground of Christian living demands that he have a **Bible-saturated** life. This is the simplest logic. There is no other way to follow Christ and out-live His likeness, because the Bible is **GOD'S ONLY REVELATION OF CHRIST.**

PRINCIPLES BASIC TO THE MATTER OF DIVORCE

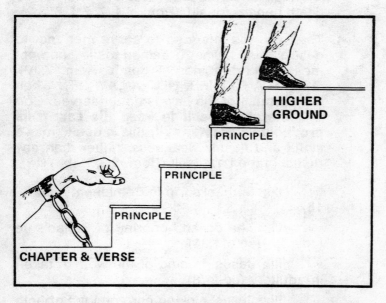

Here are the biblical principles encountered thus far in considering; (1) God's heart, (2) the Law, (3) man's sinful condition. Together, they resolve the divorce difficulty:

1. The **letter** of the Law is a vehicle which carries the **message** of the Law. The Law itself is spiritual, coming to man in words (Rom. 7:14).

93

The words communicate the message of life, but they are **not** the message itself.

2. The letter of the Law (actual wording) becomes a **killer** when imposed upon sinful men who cannot keep it (2 Cor. 3:6). God desires that men serve the spirit of the Law (its intent) and not the letter (Rom. 7:6).

3. The only escape for man under the Law is through the death of Christ. Receiving Christ's death as one's own, places him beyond the jurisdiction of the Law, out of reach of its death penalty for sin. (Rom. 6:4, 7; 7:4, 6; 8:2).

4. The Law was intended to **serve** man, not to destroy him. It was "ordained to life," and not meant to bring eternal death (Rom. 7:10). GOD IS A FATHER, NOT A LAWYER. When the **purpose** of the Law is better served, God will **tolerate an evil to keep His Law from producing a greater evil;** this is due to man's sinful and fleshly weakness, rather than any defect in the Law itself (Rom. 8:3; Heb. 7:18).

       Ill.: Samuel's trip to Bethlehem (1 Sam. 16).

       Ill.: The divine honoring of Rahab's lie (Jos. 2; Heb. 11:31).

       Ill.: Jesus' freeing of the woman taken in adultery (John 8).

       Ill.: Jesus' picking corn on the Sabbath (Mk. 2:23-28).

       Ill.: Jesus' reference to David's eating of the shewbread to teach the heart obedience principle (Mk. 2:25,26).

       Ill.: God's own command to slay entire nations in direct opposition to the sixth commandment (1 Sam. 15:3).

5. Real obedience to God's Law is from the heart (Rom. 6:16). This is not only because the "Law is spiritual," but because it is the very place where it is disobeyed.

   Ill.: Adultery is committed within the heart (Matt. 5:28).

   Ill.: Murder is in the heart (1 John 3:15). Physical murder is merely hatred in action.

6. God looks upon the **heart** of an individual to determine his obedience, while man's vision is limited to **external behavior.** The outward actions may or may not reflect the inward condition (1 Sam. 16:7). Human judgments are based upon observing external acts. God's judgments consider one's inner thoughts.

7. No man, other than Jesus, has been able to **fulfill** even one of the commandments of the Law, particularly the first. To offend the Law at any point, is to be **guilty of all of it** (Jas. 2:10; Gal. 3:10). Every person has offended the Law, for there is none righteous. The only way the Law can be kept, whether in New Testament form or Old, is through faith in Christ.

8. Christians err when they apply the LETTER OF EITHER TESTAMENT against one another as a standard or measure of personal righteousness. Since righteousness is by faith, the correct way to judge a person, is to behold his faith. Only God can do that. To weigh **exposed sins** (only kind knowable) against biblical verses is not only unfair, but renders errant judgments (Rom. 5:1; Matt. 7:5). At best, human judgments are wide of the mark, for only God knows the real intent of

the heart. Since no Christian can keep the letter of the New Testament, for one to judge another **legally** amounts to the "pot calling the kettle black."

CONCLUSION

These principles offer that the only way the marriage law can be obeyed is from the heart. Marriage is a wedding of hearts, not a joining of bodies. The Law is not fulfilled through the performing of ceremonies, inasmuch as they are external representations which easily disguise the real truth. Divorce is a matter of the heart. God beholds the inward disunion long before men witness its legal manifestation (court action). Many Christians are already divorced in the sight of God, even though their heart disunion has not been confirmed publicly — God alone being aware of their adulterous state. The recognition of these truths strips away the desire to condemn those whose divorced state is exposed.

Chapter Six

USING THE PRINCIPLES IN A DIVORCE SITUATION

Volumes have been written to show the distinction between separation, divorce and remarriage. Some writers argue that Christians may separate but must not divorce. Others say divorce is permissible under certain conditions, but the Christian must not remarry. When we consider the basic truth of Jesus' sermon on the mount, we will see that these three actions are but **different expressions of the same disorder.** The Lord's sermon reaffirmed the fact that God looks on men's hearts to appraise their lives, rather than their outward acts.

We clarify the matter with a question: "When does a bank robber become a bank robber?" Think about that. Does he become a bank robber when he produces a gun and demands the teller's money? Or is it when he first walks through the door of the

97

bank? Should we back up to when he got out of his car to enter the bank? We can back up further to when he picked up his gun and mask to head for the bank. But that's not when it happened either. We can even go back to when he was lying in bed planning the holdup, but none of these really made him a bank robber. It occurred the moment he DECIDED to pull the job.

A bank robber became a bank robber the moment he DECIDED to pull the job.

In the split second when he chose to commit the crime he became a bank robber in the sight of God. His thoughts fathered the deed. What he did following his decision were simply **different steps** in the one and **same crime.** Once he elected to become a bank robber, all of his actions after that were but various forms of the same offense.

This is the kind of thinking the Lord asked of His disciples as He taught them that anger, hatred and murder were simply **different expressions** of the same sin. The problem lies in the **heart** of the sinner.

Anything that comes as a result of his heart condition is simply a manifestation of his inner wickedness (Matt. 5:21-22). The same is true of separation, divorce and remarriage. When we view them from the heart level, as God does, we see that separation is but one evidence of the inward heart disunion. Divorce (legal) is merely a by-product of the separation, while remarriage is the final form of the same problem. The three actions are merely different expressions of the same disorder.

Consequently we should not distinguish between separation, divorce and remarriage. Theologians love to debate these things, but they have no bearing on the matter. If we will do that, then we're free to face the more urgent problem — determining WHICH of the three forms is best suited to a person's situation.

THE PRINCIPLES PROVIDE A SCRIPTURAL APPROACH TO DIVORCE

Equipped with the knowledge of God's operating principles, a person can consider the divorce question differently than one who limits himself to the "chapter and verse" approach. His outlook is totally different. He feels different about it. The difference between the two approaches lies in the fact that the "principle" approach regards God's Word as a REVELATION, whereas "chapter and verse" approach regards God's Word as a RULE BOOK.

Yet it is not enough to **know** God's principles, a person must also know how to USE them. If you had a very fine piano but were unable to play it, it would be of little value to you. The same would be true of having an expensive automobile without knowing how to drive. Therefore we need to learn HOW God's principles apply to divorce. I will give you a five-step plan for thinking through a divorce situation.

Not knowing how to use God's operating principles is like having a very fine piano and unable to play it.

NOTE. We don't have to say much about INVOLUNTARY separation. When the separation of the partners is beyond the Christian's control, he can assume the Lord has caused it. The Scriptural warrant, "What God hath joined let not man put asunder," does not prevent the Lord Himself from doing so. In His wisdom He might indeed separate two people. Auto accidents, fatal illnesses, long prison terms are but a few of the devices God might use to end a physical union. Even if the unsaved mate simply walks away from the marriage, the believing partner is not to be upset. Paul makes that clear: "If the unbelieving one leaves, LET HIM LEAVE, the brother or sister is not under bondage in such cases . . ." (1 Cor. 7:15). The believer can have perfect peace in that situation, for the matter is out of his hands. There are no choices confronting him.

Those facing marital disunion have four choices open to them:

(1) Remain in the situation and do nothing.

(2) Consider separation.

(3) Take divorce action.

(4) Remarry.

STEP ONE: SHOULD A SEPARATION BE CONSIDERED?

There are numerous situations which might cause one to consider leaving his or her mate. Dope addiction is common today.

There are numerous situations which might cause one to consider leaving his or her mate. Dope addiction and sexual perversion are common today, as are alcoholism and brutality. Temper, sexual incompatability and extreme selfishness can cause hearts to drift apart. When these things continue for years, they can KILL the love one has for another. With love gone, a spiritual divorce has already occurred. A legal divorce would simply be the outward manifestation of the inward disunion. However, before a Christian considers divorce he should ask himself three questions:

1. Has our marriage really been dissolved at the heart level?

2. Is it within my power to effect a spiritual reunion through a deeper commitment to the Lord and a change in my behavior?

3. Am I willing to give the Lord a chance to do what He can through me to make sure the separation is not of my own doing?

Unless a Christian can answer those questions to his own satisfaction he should not consider a divorce. For believers to forsake their partners merely because they can't get along is no solution. That is defeat. The very concept of Christian victory implies a **Christian fight.** Until a person has worked hard to be the kind of a mate he should be, divorce ought to be out of the question. Those who run because they find it too difficult to live with a certain person, generally find they haven't escaped the problem. The difficulty lies within them, so that no matter how much they run, they take the problem with them.

For those seeking an escape from boredom, dissatisfaction, and self-denial, divorce is not the answer. They should seek a spiritual solution. These people need to surrender to the Holy Spirit and let

Him show them how to overcome their boredom through serving Christ in the marriage. Those needing to learn how to yield themselves in marriage, will never learn it by running to other mates. Taking a new mate or changing the outward circumstances is never a substitute for surrender to the Spirit of God. Until a Christian has done his best to be the kind of a mate God wants him to be, he is in no position to consider divorce.

For those seeking an escape from dissatisfaction, divorce is not the answer. Trading one wife for another is never a substitute for surrender to God's will.

NOTE. Sometimes marriage counselors will recommend a temporary separation. When the partners have been picking at each other for so long, they reach the place where they can stir up feelings with a single look. When the situation reaches that point, they are in no condition to make a decision about their marriage. They can't think straight. But if they will separate long enough to give their feelings a chance to die down, they can then take a look at their marriage to see if it is worth saving. A separation for the purpose of reexamining the lovely privilege of living together is one tool of the marriage counselor.

STEP TWO: IS THE SITUATION MAKING YOU BITTER OR BETTER?

Those two words may sound alike, but they are opposites. They hold the KEY in determining whether or not Christians should dissolve their marriages. If the marriage is making a person sweeter and more tender, that is, more like Jesus, then it is accomplishing God's will. Divorce is out of the question when marital pressures serve to shape one in the likeness of the Lord. On the other hand, if the marital pressures are making the believer bitter towards his mate, turning him into a hard, vengeful person, then it is frustrating the purpose of God. He is becoming **unlike** the Lord.

Consider what God thinks of that marriage where the partners are changing **for the worse.** What does He want then? Does He mean for the marriage to survive at the expense of the people? Does He want that marriage to stand even if the couple inside the marriage collapses? **Definitely not!** That would make God a Lawyer rather than a Father. He would be more interested in the technicalities of the Law than the plight of His people. Marriage is sacred, holy and important. But it is not **that** important to God. He doesn't sacrifice people for a program. That is contrary to all we know about Him. He loves **people,** not programs.

When a marriage begins to destroy the very one it is supposed to build, it's time for another look at that marriage — **but from God's point of view.** Our motive is right when we see as God sees and feel as God feels. Consider the Lord Jesus and what He said when taken to task for plucking corn on the Sabbath ... "The Sabbath was made for man, man was not made for the Sabbath!" (Mark 2:27). That same principle applies here. **Marriage was made for man, man was not made for marriage!** This is a vital point. People do not exist for the sake of marriage. Marriage exists for their benefit. So then, the key to separation or divorce is found in the answer to this question:

"Is my marriage making me bitter or better — **in the sight of God?"**

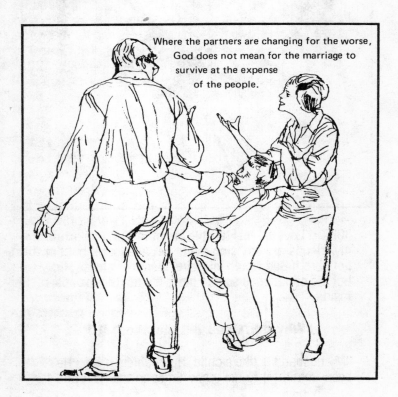

Where the partners are changing for the worse, God does not mean for the marriage to survive at the expense of the people.

Here's a case. This lady telephoned from the Midwest:

"Dr. Lovett, my husband is like a child."

"Oh Dr. Lovett, I feel terrible about this. My folks and my friends are advising me to get a divorce, but I'm not sure if God would approve. I want to please Him, but the situation is so bad here, it's tearing me apart inside."

"Why don't you tell me about it."

"My husband is like a child. His problem is sex. He's been unfaithful to me many times in the past and I have always forgiven him. But now he's living with a woman who is no good. She's got four children of her own and he refuses to help with our children. We have three and the youngest is ten. He says he doesn't love me anymore, and if I want a divorce I should go ahead and get it."

"Do you still love him?"

"I did for a long time. But now that he flaunts this woman in my face and tells me he wants nothing to do with me, I'm afraid my love has turned to hate. It's making me physically sick. We're on state aid and my days are a living hell. I'm filled with so much bitterness and resentment, I find myself wishing he would die or get killed. I've even thought of killing him myself. I'd kill myself, but who'd take care of the children?"

When I heard that, I knew the marriage was destroying this woman. It was clear to me that she should separate herself from this man and make a life for herself apart from him. However, you don't give that kind of advice over the phone on the basis of a single call. So I told her I would send her a book that would show her how to weigh the matter before the Lord and come to a decision acceptable to Him. I mailed her a copy of **The Compassionate Side Of Divorce.** That way she could weigh the matter and come to a decision on her own.

Marriage can be dangerous. It can seriously damage a person's spirit. If your marriage is producing satanic feelings in you, it could be dangerous. It is possible to receive an injury in marriage from which you will never recover. By never, I mean the damage accompanies you into heaven. If you become a bitter, hostile person as the result of living with a mate, your marriage has changed your personality for the worse. If you do nothing to stop the

107

ungodly changes taking place in you, you will find yourself becoming less and less like Jesus. If death should find you like that, you will enter heaven just as you are — and never change.

NEVER CHANGE. I know that can be a startling idea, but it is true. However when I say you will enter heaven as you are, I do not mean that you will arrive there as a bitter and hostile person still having your old nature. The old nature stays with the flesh at physical death. It would be unthinkable that you would enter heaven that way. What I mean is this: our growth in the likeness of Christ STOPS when we die. However much we have matured to be like our Lord, that is the way we enter heaven. And our growth stops at that point. Why? The conditions for making changes in us do not exist in heaven. They are a part of this life only. For example, a man will not be able to acquire more patience in heaven. The anxiety situations needed to produce patience in a person are not found there. Long-suffering is another trait we cannot acquire in heaven. We have to be in a situation that requires us to suffer a long time in order to become long-suffering, and there is no suffering in heaven. If you are interested in the complete story on how we have but this one life in which to get ready for heaven and be like Christ, you will want to read my book, **Jesus Is Coming — Get Ready Christian!** It will shock you and motivate you to use each day to become more like Christ. This is why I say that a marital situation which makes you hostile and bitter (unlike Christ) can damage you eternally. Since we enter heaven as we are at the point of death – and never change – it is awful to permit a marriage to be the means of stunting one's growth in Christ.

So this is not an insignificant matter. When marriage, which God intends to help us become

108

more Christ-like, actually does the reverse, it is folly to stay in the situation and let yourself be damaged, especially when you consider that damage can be eternal. More than one Christian woman has been hurt in this fashion because she made herself go on living with an unsaved man. Social pressures, scruples based on mistaken notions of God's Word, financial security, habit and bad advice are a few of the many reasons why a wife will continue to live with a heathen husband even though the marriage is doing awful damage to her spirit.

NOTE. Many Christian women marry unsaved men hoping they will come to Christ and change. I'm sure you know of such cases yourself. Also you know the heartache they suffer. Then there are those women who are saved after they are married, but their husbands refuse to accept the Lord. When that happens, the wife is unequally yoked and she stays that way until her mate decides to receive Christ – if he ever does. Once a woman becomes excited about Christ and starts to live a godly life, the husband can be disappointed with her. If she changes too much he can become hostile toward the Gospel and make life miserable for her. Depending on how she reacts to this situation, she will become either BITTER or BETTER.

That's the key.

You've been to weddings. You've heard the preacher say. . .

". . . to join this man and this woman together . . . in accordance with God's holy Word; and therefore is not by any to be entered into unadvisedly or lightly; but reverently, advisedly and in the fear of God."

See those words, "advisedly" and "in the fear of

God?" Marriage is no light matter. People ought to weigh carefully what they're doing, for it can put the fear of God into them when a marriage goes sour.

"... is not by any to be entered into unadvisedly or lightly; but reverently, advisedly and in the fear of God."

Christians are not exempt from marital pressures. They make mistakes like everyone else. It happens more often than we care to admit that a godly woman marries an ungodly man and lives to regret it. There are things she can do, of course, as a Christian, to USE the pressures of marriage to break her husband's shell. But this takes knowledge and a close walk with the Lord. For those who find themselves in this situation I recommend my book, **Unequally Yoked Wives.** It sets forth a plan for using the pressures within the marriage to bring your husband to Christ. If a Christian wife is living under the same roof with her mate, she ought to try this plan BEFORE she decides to leave him.

This godly lady was married to a man addicted to alcohol.

Here's another case. This godly lady was married to a man addicted to alcohol. He would squander nearly his whole salary in bars before he got home with his paycheck. As a result the family was destitute. I could feel the agony in the poor woman's voice when she called for advice.

"What shall I do, Dr. Lovett? This has been going on for some time now. We live in a small town and everyone knows about it. I've lost what pride I had accepting charity from others. My husband is such a boy. He never grew up and it is hard for him to face reality. I guess it makes him feel like a man to drink with the fellows. But does the Lord mean for us to go on like this? Almost everyone tells me I've taken more than I should and that I ought to leave him."

"How do you feel about your husband?"

"He can be a nice person at times, but he does have a temper. He's not a Christian. I can't mention the Lord to him. He gets mad every time I do. He doesn't want to see a Bible around the house. So far he hasn't forbidden the children and me to go to church. It'd be awful if he did that, for I don't know what I'd do without those dear people standing by me."

"What is your marriage doing to you as a person? I mean, is it making you resentful? Do you find yourself hating your husband?"

"Oh no, I don't hate him. I feel sorry for him. One thing is sure, it has put me on my knees. As long as the Lord gives the grace I think I can bear it."

From the way she spoke of her husband and the Lord, I could see the marriage was NOT destroying this woman. Yes, the situation was bad, but she wasn't bitter about it. To expose the children to a drunken father would tear at a mother's heart. But as long as it was not making her bitter, the safest course for that woman is to stay in her situation and see what THE LORD does about the husband. He is aware of her plight. If HE wanted to remove the husband, it would be easy enough for Him. Besides, suffering is NORMAL in the Christian life. It is as important to God's plan as marriage itself. Therefore suffering alone cannot be the basis for divorce. As long

112

as the woman was leaning on the Lord and becoming sweeter in the situation, there is no way for her to leave her husband.

On the other hand, if this lady had told me that she resented her husband, and that she found herself thinking of vicious and vengeful things she might do to get even with him, then I would know she was being damaged by the marriage. When that happens, the marriage itself **becomes an evil.** In that case the godly wife should FLEE from it as urgently as she would from any other evil. Here then is the principle:

When an earthly marriage, which is a TEM-PORARY situation, begins to produce ETERNAL damage in a child of God, it is time to run. Don't walk — RUN. It is dangerous to trifle with evil, particularly when that evil is your own marriage.

It's a matter of priority

Don't argue that marriage is ordained of God and therefore good; and that nothing which is good can produce evil. Of course marriage is good. But there are many wonderful things in this life which can become deadly if allowed to interfere with God's plan for the Christian. One of Satan's favorite tactics is using good things to produce evil. Consider money. In the hands of a dedicated Christian money can be used to bring honor to the Lord. But let money come between that Christian and his Lord, and it is no longer a good thing. It is then a danger.

In the same way, marriage is good and holy as long as it fulfills the divine plan. Its purpose is to prepare believers as marriage partners of the Lord Jesus (2 Cor. 11:2). But when it becomes the means

113

of making a believer an **unfit** partner of the Lord, it is at once an evil. When that happens the Christian should put his destructive marriage behind him as definitly as he would anything else that threatened his growth in Christ.

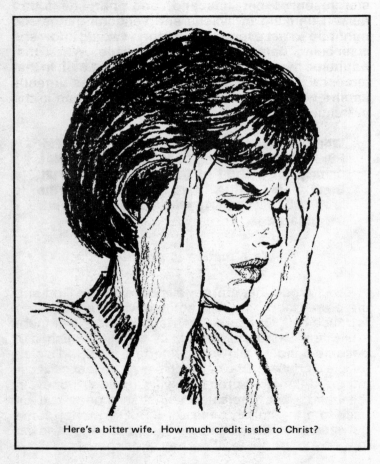

Here's a bitter wife. How much credit is she to Christ?

● Here's a bitter wife. Does her heart feel like praying? Is she in any condition to pray? Hardly. How can she talk to the Lord with bitterness flooding her soul? And what happens to her sweetness? It begins to fade. How much credit is she to Christ? None. And how will those hateful feelings, inspired by Satan, draw her close to Jesus? You know that's impossible. How then can it be God's will for a person to continue in such a situation? It just can't. The eternal purpose of God, which is Christlikeness must have the priority (Rom. 8:29). It could never be right to give the priority to earthly marriage, for that is only a TEMPORARY situation (Matt. 22:30). It would be wrong to subordinate the eternal to the temporal, for that would make marriage itself more important than the reason for which God instituted it in the first place.

STEP THREE — MAKE YOUR DECISION

Before making any decision, a believer should ask God for wisdom.

"If any of you lacks wisdom, let him ask of God, who gives to all men generously and without reproach, and it will be given to him." (James 1:5).

Before making any decision a believer should ask God for wisdom. It's foolish not to since He offers it. Wisdom is NOT an increase in mental power. It is the ability to SEE what is going on in your life with relation to the Word of God. What you are really asking of God is His help in thinking through your situation in order that you might arrive at the best solution.

HINT. In making such a decision you should be free of emotion. If you are upset with your feelings running high, that is no time to make a decision as important as this one. If it is necessary for you to get away for a few days or a week to let your emotions subside, do so. Emotion clouds reason when present in any force. If you have been suddenly called upon to speak before a group, then you know what I'm talking about. The emotional pressure is so great it makes your mind go blank. Later on, you can think of all sorts of things you wished you had said. And so it is when you try to reach a decision of this sort after quarreling or fussing with your mate. When the emotional fire dies down you can evaluate things in the light of reason.

God's operating principles are a part of the knowledge you'll be using to study the matter. It is the better part of wisdom to apply this knowledge to your situation, and free yourself from traditions and prejudices which are often more emotional than logical. The counsel of friends can be helpful as long as their thinking follows the same approach. If their suggestions are based on the "chapter and verse" approach, they will only confuse you. It would be better not to listen to them in that case.

Take your time in making the decision. Don't be fretful or anxious. God will faithfully answer your prayer for wisdom. You will soon SEE what is happening to you in your marriage. Time is the best insurance that your decision will not be made on the basis of emotion. What might seem like a long wait for God to answer your prayer for wisdom may simply be time needed to get rid of the emotional pressure built up inside you. He won't fail you. And you'll be surprised how clear it all seems when you begin to think as He does.

Take a good look at yourself. Consider what God's Word expects of you in the way of maturity. Is your marriage helping or hindering your progress in Christ? That's the goal. It should be easy to SEE that maturity in Christ means more to God than determined coexistence with a mate who is damaging your personality. It's your personality, isn't it, that you take into heaven.

When waves of ungodly feelings sweep over your spirit, when hateful and vengeful ideas are entertained in your mind, the situation cannot be allowed to go on. If you see yourself becoming BITTER rather than BETTER . . . you can't afford to remain in the situation. On the other hand, if you are becoming SWEETER and more like Christ because of the trials created by your marriage, then you can't afford to leave your mate. You are becoming rich toward God. You don't want to throw away the privilege of being conditioned for Christ. Divorce would be a mistake if the marriage situation is turning you into a sweet, gentle Christian.

Make your decision. Either way it could be painful. But you must make it. If you come to it carefully and in a calculating manner, as I have suggested, it will surface in your mind as a settled **conviction.** However there is something you need to do with this decision BEFORE carrying it out — **test it for God's approval.**

STEP FOUR: TEST DECISION FOR DIVINE APPROVAL

"If I make a decision based on reason alone, how can I be sure my choice is in the will of God?"

We've reached the place where someone might ask that. It brings us to the fourth step in the process. God has a wonderful way of letting us know whether or not He approves of our decisions. It works much the same as His granting of wisdom. Only in this case He lets us know how HE FEELS about our choice. A believer seeking to do the will of God will experience either FEAR or PEACE in connection with his decision. These two feelings are indicators which tell us whether God approves or disapproves our decision.

Both fear and peace can be FELT. They are not reasoned. These feelings arise from within the unconscious, the area where the Holy Spirit operates. He functions in this area purposely, so as not to interfere with our free wills. As a result, we do not hear His voice, neither do we experience spine-tingling sensations. Instead we simply feel comfortable about our decision, or we feel terribly uneasy. The apostle put it like this:

"Let the peace of God RULE in your hearts . . ." (Col. 3:15).

NOTE. We should distinguish between the peace OF GOD and peace WITH GOD. Peace **with** God is what we feel when we are saved. The war between us and Him is over. The enmity God has toward those outside of Christ rests on us until we receive Christ as

118

Savior (John 3:36). When we turn to Jesus, that war is over and a state of peace exists. But that is **not** the peace of which we speak here. The peace OF GOD is the inner tranquility a Christian feels when he knows he is in God's will and that everything is fine between him and the Lord. It is that peace which comes when you are sure the fellowship between you and Jesus is in no way strained or stressed. Nothing can disturb a Christian when he knows he is in the center of God's will. It is, in fact, a place of rest.

The PEACE OF GOD is a feeling. When we are out of God's will, the Holy Spirit lets us know it. We feel miserable. In fact, it would be unjust of God to let us feel comfortable if we were in any kind of spiritual danger. He won't do that. So when we have made a decision that will take us outside of His will, the Holy Spirit begins to express **His concern** within our spirit. From within our unconscious, the conviction arises . . . "This thing is wrong." As we harken to this inner voice we sense how God feels. That is why peace can exercise RULE or DOMINION over our hearts. It is a dependable guide. The Holy Spirit never deceives us in transmitting the feelings of God. Consequently we have an unfailing device for knowing whether God approves our decision or not. This peace is the key to abiding in the Father's will.

Therefore, once you have made your decision to separate from your mate, the next step is to present that decision to God in prayer. As you go to Him, be ready to do His will. If He doesn't want you to get a divorce, then you don't want it. What you are doing is checking to see what HE wants. But you must make your decision first. That's the way God does everything. We move then He moves. He never gives His blessing or indications IN ADVANCE. As you talk to Him, say:

"Dear Father, I've thought this thing through the best I could. Using the principles I've learned from this book, I find I have the liberty to separate from _____ . But it is not a matter of doing my will. I want Your will. I am ready to go either way and do what pleases You!"

Then you wait. The real test will come that night. As you lie on your bed, you will either be peaceful or toss and turn in terrible unrest. Check again and see how you feel the next day. Does your spirit pain you? Do seizures of uneasiness sweep over you? Or is there a settled assurance that even though what you face is unpleasant, it has to be done, and your soul is not unduly exercised?

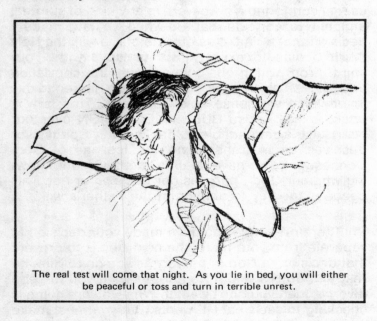

The real test will come that night. As you lie in bed, you will either be peaceful or toss and turn in terrible unrest.

NOTE. Don't confuse concern for your future with God's witness concerning your decision. Try and isolate, if you can, your concern for your personal welfare and focus on how you feel about carrying out your decision before the Lord. It's how you feel **about your decision** that counts, not how you are going to solve your problems. Those are two separate matters. To mix them will confuse you. All you are interested in at the moment is how the Lord feels about breaking up this marriage. Your outward circumstances could be awful, yet you could still feel at rest within your spirit. That is the way the peace of God works. It is wholly apart from circumstances.

Now when I say check your feelings, you must be aware that Satan will attempt to arouse worry within you. He will try to hide or cloak God's true witness, by getting you to worry about this or that happening. When that is the case, you must deal with the devil to clear the air. You simply can't get a good indication of God's will with Satan confounding the Spirit's witness with worry. This is no slight matter. If you want to be sure of the PEACE/FEAR indicators, you must be free of satanic influence. The only way to do it is to resist Satan in the power of Jesus' name. James tells us this is a definite act . . . "Resist the devil and he will flee from you" . . . (Ja. 4:7).

Someone might say, **"But I don't feel anything!"** All right, then you have nothing to fear. This means God is leaving the matter in your hands. It is not uncommon for Him to do this. You can be sure that if you were in any kind of spiritual danger, He'd never let you go into it without a warning. No human parent would do that, let alone our heavenly Father. What this means is that EITHER CHOICE is okay with Him. And He is ready to use **either decision** to bring out the best in your life. That's the greatness of our God. He is not always limited to a single choice. With His genius and wisdom He can sometimes take either decision and make it accomplish His purpose. So

121

when there is a lack of assurance, don't be concerned. All it takes to be in the will of God is the DETERMINATION to be there. If you have that determination, don't worry about getting out of His will. He won't let you. This is one of the wonders of living for Christ. There is no way to miss!

STEP FIVE: CARRY OUT THE DECISION BY FAITH.

If you have made your decision and tested it for God's will, then be at peace in the matter of separating from your mate. Sure there will be anxious moments, pangs of remorse and tinges of distress as you think of the past. **Do not interpret these as coming from God.** They are natural impulses which often follow in the wake of marital crises. In spite of them, you should have a generally relaxed feeling about your decision. It is rare for a Christian's decision to be overruled by the Lord. This is particularly so in the case of the mature Christian who has served the Lord over a period of years.

Now — if you have been deceiving yourself as you weighed your situation, seeking only to escape an unpleasant marriage rather than be in the center of God's will, then you could be miserable. There is no way for God to grant peace in a decision He cannot accept. If He did, He would compromise His faithfulness and none of us wants that. If He could compromise in His witness, He might compromise in something far more serious — our salvation.

But let's assume you are enjoying God's PEACE in the matter of your separation. It now becomes an act of faith for you to carry out your decision wholeheartedly. It will be a powerful testimony to His grace when you do this. It shows that God has accepted you and your decision. Men can debate doctrines and challenge each other's beliefs, but there is no way to deny the power of a holy, Christ-centered life. A decision to secure a divorce, joyously executed **as unto the Lord** cannot be refuted. The legalistic words of some Christians (who do not have your liberty) will fall harmlessly to the ground. They are no match for the power of God seen in your life. It is a marvelous thing to be able to honor the Lord Jesus with this kind of faith.

Satan won't like it.

If you find it hard to make your decision to proceed with a divorce, you might find it harder to live it. Satan will do all he can to dilute your victory. He is afraid of the power that will be in your life because of your faith. And He knows that others could be influenced by your example to live boldly what they believe God approves. The devil has powerful weapons. Worry, fear, discouragement can come into your life as Satan stirs up people close to you, people whom you respect, to attack you. The devil likes to use men of God, people who know the Word but not God's heart, because their hurt is particularly painful. When your pastor takes a stand against you, you'll feel it. It may happen. But if I tell you ahead of time, the hurt won't be so great now that you are prepared to meet it.

The divorced Christian must not become bitter toward those who don't share his view of God's graciousness. He should stretch his heart and try to understand that they are immature, lacking the faith to appropriate this kind of liberty in Christ. The apostle Paul refers to such Christians as weak in faith (Rom. 14:2). They may be pastors or old time Bible students, but they are still weak in faith when it comes to exercising the "glorious liberty of the sons of God!" It is wrong for you to scorn them, it is wrong

123

for them to judge you. This is the essense of Paul's teaching in the fourteenth chapter of Romans.

Now when Satan strikes a dampening blow at your victory, you'll find yourself thinking, "Did I do the right thing? I wonder if God is really as gracious as I have made Him out to be? Am I wrong to take this step when so many feel divorce is unthinkable for Christians?" These are things Satan will try to plant in your mind. Don't let him get away with it. If you buy his suggestions, you'll start thinking your life is ruined and you are useless to God. That is false. If I warn you ahead of time you will be ready when he tries to put such doubts in your mind. When he does, simply tell him to "bug off," and remember that God is a Father and not a Lawyer. He wants to use your life and He'll take it any way He can get it — as long as you love Him and seek to do His will. No matter what other Christians might tell you, there is no limit to what God can do with the divorced believer who sets His heart on pleasing the Lord. Divorced or not, God can use you as mightily as any pastor or missionary or evangelist. That's the kind of a God we serve. His strength is made perfect in our weakness.

MEETING SATAN'S ATTACKS

When doubts and fears rise within you and words of condemnation come from the outside, be mature enough to realize that Satan is the attacker and not those individuals he is using to communicate his treachery. The Lord wants us to love those brethren who bring discomfort and condemnation, even though we HATE the one using them. There are three things you can do to thwart Satan's attacks:

1 Resist the devil himself. I alluded to this earlier, now we are ready to consider direct action

124

against Satan. The Lord Jesus is our example. When He was attacked by Satan He spoke to him directly. He ordered him away, using the Word of God as a weapon. We can do the same. In fact, we are told precisely to . . . "Resist the devil and he will flee from you" (James 4:7). The apostle Paul exhorts us to take a stand against Satan and deal with him (Eph. 6:11, 12). When we do, he will flee from us. He is already a defeated enemy. When ordered away in Jesus' name, he must go. If the idea of dealing with Satan and taking authority over him is new to you, then you will profit greatly from my book, **Dealing with the Devil.** It sets forth a four-step plan for putting him to flight. You can use it the moment you read it. And it really works. He does go. And when he does, those doubts and pressures ease at once.

The Apostle Paul exhorts us to take a stand against Satan and to deal with him.

Turn to God's Word for refreshment.

2 Turn to God's Word for refreshment. There are a number of passages where the PRINCIPLE approach is spelled out in a single verse. Romans 14:14 is significant; "I know and am persuaded by the Lord Jesus that nothing is unclean of itself ..." That applies to divorce as well as anything else. If Christians were under the Law, they'd find many things listed as unclean. But when a man comes to Christ, he is totally liberated from the letter of the Law. He finds that the only time anything is unclean is when he THINKS it is unclean. Here's the whole verse:

"I know and am persuaded by the Lord Jesus that nothing is unclean of itself; but to him who thinks anything is unclean, to him it is unclean."

There are those who think separation, divorce and remarriage are unclean. All right, if they think so, then to them it IS unclean. But to those who realize that evil does NOT EXIST IN THINGS, but only in one's attitude toward them — these are not unclean at all. Evil resides in the heart, not in things. This is why Paul went on to say, **"the faith that you have, have as your own conviction before God. Happy is he who does not condemn himself in what he approves"** (Rom. 14:22). It's a glorious thing to be free of traditions of men and the RULES of the letter of the Law. Only those who are mature in Christ have this freedom. So relax in the sure knowledge that if you have the faith to appropriate your liberty in Christ, you will not fall. The apostle Paul knows that those who rise to this level of freedom are often concerned with what others think. But the Word guarantees that the man who lives to please the Lord and who uses his freedom IN THE LORD **will stand** (Vs. 4). If God is pleased with your decision, He can make you stand no matter what other people might think.

There is another principle spelled out in the Word of God that offers a word of comfort to the divorced: **"We know that God causes all things to work together for good to those who love God, to those who are called according to His purpose"** (Rom. 8:28). Can you fathom the significance of that verse? It's an entire principle. Even if your divorce was a MISTAKE . . . God can still make it work for your good and His eternal purpose. As long as your heart yearns to please Him, there is no way to miss. If you set your heart to do His will, this verse guarantees you will not — no, you **cannot** get out of His will. It is impossible. See, New Testament christianity always boils down to the heart of the believer. There are some who won't like this kind of freedom. They call it license. But it's not. This is a higher level of faith and not everyone in Christ attains to it. Those who don't, tend to JUDGE those who do. The apostle Paul is quite forceful in exhorting WEAK Christians not to judge those who have such liberty in the Lord (Rom. 14:4).

Reassure yourself in the Lord's presence.

3 Reassure yourself in the Lord's presence. It is the Lord who is to judge you, not other Christians. The sweetest kind of assurance sweeps over your spirit when you know that you and your decision are accepted by Him. If you have even the slightest concern regarding your decision, go to prayer. The devil, of course, will try to substitute ungodly fear in the place of the peace God has given you. That's why you must order him away. Then, as you fellowship with the Lord Jesus, you feel His approval. If you want to, go over the whole thing with

Him again. Ask for His indication to your heart once more. As you think of the Scriptures I've given you, the principles by which God operates, plus the fact that you have done your best to be sure your decision has His approval, the peace of God should settle over your soul. Then you will know everything is all right between you and Him. If God is for you, who can be against you?

So now you don't have to worry about Satan. Neither do you have to cringe before over-zealous, but weaker Christians. Relax. Bask in the assurance that God has already fitted your divorce into His plan for your life and is ready to use it for His glory. When you have that kind of assurance, the devil's attacks fall harmlessly to the ground.

HOW THIS HELPS THOSE WHO ARE DIVORCED

As you read this book, does it now appear that you made a mistake in dissolving your marriage? Don't be upset. All you have to do is be ready to do what God wants you to do and all will be well. To suddenly decide to return to your original partner would be wrong. You could be adding one mistake on top of another. Just because you discover a mistake is not sufficient reason for going backwards.

You must treat that possibility in the same way as though you were getting a divorce. That is, you need to weigh it and see whether or not the situation would make you **bitter or better** before the Lord. Don't act hastily. If your former mate has since remarried, you could damage others by trying to engineer a reunion. You must first check with the Lord to see if such a move is in His will. It is probable that God would NOT have you go back. Yet there is nothing wrong in going through all the steps and testing for His approval. If the circumstances are favorable and you secure God's witness that He approves the decision, then you could proceed to remarry your mate. But the important thing is checking for God's approval.

> **NOTE.** It bears repeating that while Christians are set free from traditions and the letter of the Law, they are NOT free to live as they please. That is license. They are free only to please the Lord. The Lordship of Christ is the overall guiding principle for the believer. What the Christian is free to do is this: he can do anything he likes to **please the Lord.** This is why Paul says, "Whatever you do in word or deed do all in the name of the Lord Jesus, giving thanks through Him to God the Father" (Col. 3:17). Believers are free only to do that which they can do "as unto the Lord." The moment they seek to do things as unto themselves, they step out of God's will. Our freedom must be exercised by faith (with thanksgiving) for whatsoever is not of faith – **is sin.** While we have enormous liberty in Christ, it cannot be used to please the flesh. It must all be used to bring honor and pleasure to Jesus. He owns us lock, stock and barrel having bought us at the price of His own blood. Therefore we are obliged to live for Him rather than ourselves. (2 Cor. 5:15).

• Perhaps those helped most by this approach are those believers who later realize they were responsible for the failure of the marriage in the first place. They now see how their marriage could have been saved had they been closer to the Lord and been more submissive to Him. But the divorce has occurred. It's done now, and there is no way to undo it. These people suffer. They are plagued with guilts which are in turn reinforced by the opinions of others as well as the severe stand of their church. It is to these people that this approach brings the greatest relief.

It is a fantastic thing to learn that God accepts you **as you are** — right now. If your heart is set to please Him from now on, the past doesn't matter. Sure it was wrong to get the divorce in the first place, but what is that to God? He is big enough and wise enough to take any life that truly loves Him and bring that person to his full potential in Christ. No matter what our mistakes, "the blood of Jesus Christ, God's Son, keeps on cleansing us from ALL sin" (1st John 1:7). The past is washed away by the blood of Jesus and a new day beckons those divorcees who want to exalt Christ. Regardless of what weaker Christians think, there is no limit to what God can do with a Christ-honoring divorce or divorcee. "If God be for us, WHO can be against us?" (Rom. 8:31). All a divorced Christian has to do is bow before God and say:

> **"Lord, I'm sorry I made a mistake in getting that divorce. I was wrong. I admit it. But I give my life to you and I am ready to walk in the light of your Word. Henceforth I dedicate myself to You. I am ready to live before You. I want to please You and I am ready to do what You ask of me. In Jesus' name. Amen."**

If you can give yourself to the Lord like that, then forget about that divorce. God has! It will not be a barrier to your becoming rich in the Lord or in serving Him. He can use you in ways you never dreamed. Even if you can't hold a position in some church, so what? God has thousands of ways of using those who mean business for Him. He will give you the fullness of His Spirit and set before you an open door which no man can close. (Rev. 3:8).

Chapter Seven

HEALING FOR DIVORCE

Individuals usually fall into three classes with respect to the divorce question: (1) Those already divorced, (2) those facing a divorce situation, and (3) those in close contact with divorced persons and wondering as to the proper Christian stand. It is to these people that our principles bring the most help.

Those already divorced. Many a divorced Christian suffers untold anguish and heartache because of his divorce record. Not only does he suffer condemnation and judgment from others, but he frequently bears depressing guilts. Learning of God's attitude toward sinful man and His method of dealing with divorce can bring release from these guilt feelings.

The release comes when it is discovered that

God is not a condemning person. He is most sympathetic and tolerant of the divorcee, for He views the heart rather than one's acts. When the heart is **set** to please God, then regardless of any acts, that person is considered PERFECT by God. David is a splendid example — this famous **murderer - adulterer** of the Old Testament declared, "I saw the Lord always before my face, for He is at my right hand that I should not be moved" (Acts 2:25). There was Lot too, who apparently **preferred** the dreadful wickedness of the city of Sodom to fellowship with God's people, yet Peter found him to be a "righteous man" (2 Pet. 2:8).

Coming to know how God really feels permits one to enjoy complete release from any guilt in connection with his divorce. God's heart is not marred by reservations or feelings of judgment. His forgiveness is complete, His cleansing thorough. The heart of a man is what really counts in the sight of God — **not his history.**

It is an act of faith to accept God's complete pardon through Christ and to proceed as though one had never been divorced at all. To move among Christians as though no divorce had occurred is to offer living proof of one's faith in God's willingness to **utterly** forgive and cleanse. To behave otherwise, suffer guilty feelings even, is to be unaware of His goodness. The divorced person need not hesitate to step out and serve Christ. He will soon learn that God blesses obedience on the part of any of His children with startling power. **The proof of this lies in the doing.**

Those facing a divorce situation. Christians **facing** a divorce situation suffer, not so much from guilts (unless it is from wishing they could be divorced) but from a haunting theme that continually goes through their minds; "I am a Christian and Christians do not believe in divorce." The more pressure and strain that is brought upon the marriage, the louder the phrase repeats itself. These people are caught between the seemingly inflexible demands of the Bible and the intolerable nature of their marriage situation.

Some in a divorce situation shoot themselves, all because they feel bound to a rigid code.

Some in this plight shoot themselves, take overdoses of sleeping pills, suffer nervous and mental breakdowns plus a host of secondary ills, and all because they feel bound to a rigid code. When humans are caught between an inhuman standard and a superhuman situation, something has to yield. Usually it is the human that gives way. Soul damage is the inevitable result every time people are placed under an inflexible code unless some "way of escape" is provided.

The way of escape for Christians suffering an intolerable marriage situation is the invoking of the "higher law" of marriage. When the greater good or better yet, when God's purpose in marriage can be **better served** through a divorce, then divorce is better than an attempted conformity to the code. Here I speak of legal divorce, for couples in such a situation have undoubtedly been **spiritually divorced** for some time.

When the Christian, of a clear conscience, can determine that God's purpose in marriage is better served by a civil divorce action, that way is open to him without prejudice. This does not mean that God favors divorce, only that He is pleased to accept His child's decision in the matter. It is as though He were to say, "My son, if your heart does not condemn you in this matter then neither do I condemn you. As long as you honestly feel that you are doing what I would do in your situation you can act without any fear of judgment from Me."

Of course, if the greater good could be accomplished by remaining within the marriage situation, then divorce is out of the question. The human heart is so deceptive at this point that Christians do well in seeking the help of one who truly loves the Lord and yet has insight to His purpose of marriage. The fact that a man and wife may be spiritually divorced in God's sight does **not demand** that they secure a legal divorce. Such a step could produce even greater evils. The mere presence of a spiritual divorce is not sufficient basis for a civil divorce.

Those faced with an intolerable marriage are helped by the knowledge of the two kinds of divorce — spiritual and legal. No sin is incurred by the civil process unless it produces injury to others. As far as the legal divorce itself is concerned, the action is of minor interest to God, for He has been witnessing the heart divorce all along. Thus, the principle of heart marriage and heart divorce can bring relief to marital agony. Sincere lovers of Christ can be freed from desperate situations by invoking the spirit of the law, instead of breaking neath the weight of its letter.

Those in contact with Christian divorcees. The principle of spiritual divorce and civil divorce helps a third class of individuals. The publicly divorced Christian is often deeply hurt when he suffers discrimination at the hand of the church family. Those who are the closest can bring the most hurt, and sometimes the point of the divorcee's deepest wounding is the very place where his spiritual life should flourish — in Christian fellowship. The very thing he needs most, becomes the ground of his hardest testing.

The publicly divorced Christian is often deeply hurt when he suffers discrimination at the hand of the church family.

The sincere Christian, who weighs his own stand with respect to divorced persons, finds he loses all desire to discriminate between his brethren once he lays hold of God's operating principles. His heart is changed. The power of God's truth works in his life to the place where he no longer can accept one group of people and reject the other. The awareness of the two kinds of divorce makes everything different. He turns his eyes inward to see if perchance he himself might not be living in spiritual adultery. Rather than point an accusing finger at a brother with an outward divorce record, he reappraises his own marriage and asks, "Is there really a true heart union between my wife and myself? Is ours a marriage in God's eyes or is it a mask for the eyes of our brothers? Am I myself a spiritual divorcee?" Such thoughts could come to mind when one realizes how God actually views marriage.

The possession of this knowledge brings the desire to treat all of his brethren without discrimination. Far from casting stones at those with divorce records, he finds that contact with them gives him an opportunity to be like His Savior and behave as He might. Judging less and less by outward appearances, he discovers he is able to accept the sinner, even while hating the sin. His heart reaches out with the same compassion displayed by his Master toward the woman taken in adultery, "Neither do I condemn thee." The outliving of this grace brings him to accept men as they are. The distinction of whether people are spiritually or publicly divorced no longer interferes with his love. He is **released** from that type of judgmentalism and free to help his church walk in the same light.

DIVORCE BEFORE AND AFTER SALVATION

Occasionally the thought is advanced that what

happens in a man's life before he is saved is one thing, and that which occurs after salvation is another. Sometimes it is felt that the "blood of Christ" wonderfully covers former sins committed in ignorance, but once a man accepts Christ certain things become unpardonable. Divorce is often regarded as one of these intolerable deeds. In some places, if a Christian obtains a public divorce, it is considered unforgiveable, and he is snubbed by his circle of Christian friends. It is argued that since he is saved, he knows better and has sinned in light. Also, he has failed to live out **complete** victory in the Holy Spirit.

The argument, while lofty in sound and implication, betrays a surprising ignorance of the **grace of God.** The real truth is that before people are saved they are under the Law and totally condemned; but after they are saved, they are delivered from that state to know and live by the wonderful grace of the Lord. This astonishing grace is **apart from all deeds and the Law,** and imparts **unmerited** righteousness to every Christian. This is the very meaning of grace itself.

The Christian is a **saved** sinner, but still a sinner. Those brethren who pass judgment upon others, because their sins are of a more **public** nature than their own, fail to **reveal** the wonderful grace of Jesus. It is the awareness of **secret** and **spiritual** divorce and adultery that puts an end to this dreadful practice. Often the very ones loudest in their denunciation of a brother's EXPOSED FAULT have the same sin lying unexposed in their own hearts. A person who honestly examines his heart before God and discovers the depravity that still lurks there secretly, is not so prone to condemn those who have been forced to bring theirs before the public eye. It all changes when one begins to see as God sees.

More than one Christian, who has viciously pounced upon a divorced brother, is himself living in a state of **spiritual adultery** and just as guilty as far as God is concerned. The mask of propriety, while deceiving the church family and the neighbors, makes no impression upon God. Thus, the before and after salvation distinction is an artificial one. All that happens to an individual after salvation, **as far as personal righteousness** is concerned, is that the Holy Spirit helps him grow in the likeness of Christ. Personal righteousness and the Lord's imparted righteousness are not the same. The failures of one moment are to be forgotten immediately as the Christian presses TOWARD the mark of his high call in Christ (Phil. 3:13,14). If Paul could not count himself to "have arrived," it is not likely that anyone since can make such a claim.

THE PRINCIPLES AND THE CHURCH

The position of the church as the representative of divine Law and forgiving grace, is not an easy one. Standing as the formal representative of Jesus Christ, she has felt it necessary to uphold the high standard of the original marriage law and defend TO THE LETTER its lofty tenets. It has been a valiant stand. To do otherwise seemingly compromises the holiness of God's Law.

The institution, however, is called upon to minister the grace of Christ. This dual role of upholding standards and reflecting that loving and forgiving graciousness which accepts men as they come, is not easy. It is difficult to be the minister of Mt. Sinai, with its smoking and quaking awesomeness that declares the majesty of God, and at the same time call to men from Mt. Calvary and say, "Come as you are."

The church's new freedom. The power of the Roman Church is broken once again when the principle approach is applied rather than the "chapter and verse." The church did not shake off all the evil shackles of Dark Age bondage when she came out of Roman Catholicism. There still clings the matter of **complete intolerance** in the area of divorce. The Romanists employ an "annulment" mechanism to declare a marital union "no marriage," but the Protestants have no such device until we come to God's operating principles.

"I will never perform a wedding ceremony for divorced persons!" More than one churchman has hated those words as they came from his own lips, knowing full well they do not reflect the charitable grace of Jesus. Yet, the servant's good conscience didn't permit him to put his seal to an act which he feels violates the demand of the Law. To his mind, to marry divorced people or admit them to membership, amounts to flaunting man's sinful practices in the face of God and compromising the divine standard. Even so he is not happy about his stand. His lips have been dedicated to speaking the **heart** of Christ to men. He is aware something is wrong. He knows that the real purpose of God is not being fulfilled toward the very people who need his help and ministry the most.

This is not to say that ministers can look into men's hearts — but almost that. "As a man thinketh in his heart, so is he," said Jesus. And when Christians begin to watch and listen for those things which certify one's heart condition rather than portray his weaknesses, they come closer to the divine pattern for dealing with people. Instead of "I can't marry you because of your divorce record," it now

140

becomes "Christ is waiting to help you through me. I and my people will do what we can to make you happy and help you find your greatest joy in living for Him." The basis for such a remark would not be the man's divorce record, but his heart relationship to the Lord.

This approach does not lower the standard of the church. It actually fulfills it. The **purpose** of the Law is higher than the letter, and when the purpose of the Law is fulfilled through toleration, then God's will is better accomplished than by strict adherance to the legal demand. In this way the heart of God is revealed and the Law satisfied.

What a freedom this is! Free to follow the spirit of the Law and not its letter; free from having to judge and condemn men for their deeds; free from having to measure others by legal standards — a practice which can only divide the family of God.

 **The Church's new heart.** What a thrilling thing it is when the church can extend its arms to all and say, "Come as you are and we will receive you in the name of Christ." This is the picture of Jesus that the church should present. The non-judgmental Christ cannot be pictured by a discriminating church. The whole tenor of the church program becomes sweeter. The way to fellowship and service is not barred when the principle approach brings the church a new heart. What a horrible inconsistency to say, "Come," and then throw up a barricade of thorns in the path of those with unfortunate marriage records. How many families have suffered hurt because of this ungracious procedure — to say nothing of the vast talent pool that it has idled and rusted. Many lives, bursting with gifts from

God, could be salvaged through this change of heart.

The story is even more lovely when the divorced person shares equal status with the gossipers, the hot tempered deacons and elders, and the critical church gatherers. Then all can enjoy the same brand — just plain sinners. The pastor who can marry the ex-murderer and the wire-tapper, admitting them to church office, can with equal conscience marry and even remarry divorced individuals. They then become no different than the repentant swindler who gains a high place in the church. All are found to be of the same litter and in need of Jesus' sweet presence and the transforming power of His Word. They all need fellowship and service if they are to grow. In this kind of a church, Christ is offered as the Healer of broken hearts and His ministry reaches every level. What a reputation for the church to have — it consorts with sinners, publicans and harlots. Should any church fear to have the very same reputation as its Master — gentle and tolerant, hating the sin, but loving the sinner?

SUMMARY

Individuals

The divorced Christian is released from guilts through understanding God's program to impart righteousness through faith. He finds that acts of depravity, which are the unpleasant by-products of his participation in a sinful world, do not interfere with God's love for him or **His plan** for his life. It becomes an act of faith for him to walk among other Christians as though a divorce had never occurred regardless of any **human** standards raised against him.

Christians facing divorce situations are released from both the letter of the Law and the "Dark Age" traditions which would bind them. Civil divorce is merely a manifestation of the inward divorce that has persisted in God's sight, and court action is the means of bringing a spiritually adulterous state to an end. With this wisdom the plagued Christian finds that public divorce is more in keeping with the will of God than an attempt to keep up appearances.

Church

The church enjoys a new freedom when she finds she does not have to lower her standards in receiving divorcees along with murderers and hot-tempered slanderers, for the **purpose** of holiness is better accomplished through toleration than through discrimination. She displays a new heart when she receives all men equally, as does her Lord. A new vision spreads before her when she can minister to marriage partners with counsel uncolored by divorce prejudice.

DIVORCE IS NOT NICE

The divorce problem is hard to discuss. There is some risk for the evangelical who dares to write about it, even though he brings help from the Word of God. Yet it must be done. The negative side with its accusing and indicting can't be the only stand. There is a positive side, a compassionate side. It is desperately needed. The author is ready to risk scorn to bring what help he can. At the same time, however, he knows he does not have the final word and what he presents is open to further light.

Some will say this book sanctions the breaking of the marriage vow. That is not my intention, of course. But vow-breaking is not exactly new to us. Here's a

143

Catholic priest. He breaks his vow to the church and becomes an evangelical. We have several prominent ones going about these days and we congratulate them on having done a good thing. They have severed their sacred bond with the Roman church, yet we evangelicals feel they have done right in the sight of God. We judge it an unholy union in the first place. This is not a defense for divorce, but it does suggest there is room for consistency.

This book does not attempt to whitewash divorce. It seeks only to apply God's heart to the matter. There is no doubt about it, God hates divorce. But at the same time, He loves and accepts the divorcee. Somewhere between those two ideas we find the answer. I have called it the . . .

TOLERATION PRINCIPLE.

This isn't new to us either. Consider doctors. They hate to cut off a man's arm or his leg. Yet they will not hesitate to do so in order to save his life. And our precious God, concerned about souls even though He hates divorce, will tolerate one rather than see a life destroyed in a dangerous marriage situation.

Your author is not asking the church to sanction divorce, but to be gracious to the divorcee. The real purpose of this volume is to bring relief to those already casualties of the marriage program. There are multitudes in this situation. Divorce is here - and the rate is astonishingly high among Christians.

If some of these Christians can be rescued from their doubts and recriminations, then the book has helped. If others can be salvaged and restored to useful service, then surely the Lord is pleased. But if you disagree with me, I understand. We all see things from our own frame of reference. Please though, pass up the temptation to castigate me for trying to help God's people in a hard place. This book was written at the insistence of the Holy Spirit. His urgings would not cease until it was done. May He personally lead you to those truths that help most.

Chapter Eight

DIVORCED — YET VICTORIOUS IN CHRIST!

"Brrrrnnnnnng . . ." That was my phone. A distraught woman was calling.

"Oh Dr. Lovett, I must talk to you. I feel terrible. I have just recently been divorced and it seems God can't use me anymore. I love the Lord, and this thing is tearing me apart. I'm sure God has some answer for me."

The lady came. She was a lovely Christian. She had tried very hard to make her marriage work. But things had reached the place where her sanity was at stake. On the advice of her doctor and family she went through with a divorce.

"Our church has such a rigid stand against divorced people," she said, **"that I feel like an**

146

outcast. Everyone looks at me differently now. I can't hold an office or fill any job in the church. I'm not sure I'm a member in good standing. This divorce has created a real difference between me and the other members. Is this difference going to make me useless to the Lord?"

That lady is far from being alone in the situation. There are thousands just like her. However she had the good sense to see if God had an answer for divorcees. It was a great day for her when the Lord sent her my way. It is the nature of my ministry to help ANY believer become an effective servant of the Lord. The counsel I gave this woman is the same I have given hundreds of other casualties of the marriage program. I am including it here for it really is a part of the healing for divorce. It relieves the agonizing question which tears at the heart of nearly every divorced Christian . . .

"Am I now useless to the Lord?"

CONSIDER THIS FIRST

(1) If a person is born again, and a casualty of the marriage program, he should face the fact that there are NO accidents in the lives of true believers. Everything that happens, though it seemingly comes as a result of our waywardness, stupidity or bull-headedness, fits God's plan for our lives. God chose us on the basis of His **foreknowledge.** That means our failures (including divorces) and our evils were a part of His plan before we were born.

(2) God's power and wisdom are such that He can take EVERYTHING that happens to us and make it work for our good. Does not Romans 8:28 assure us of this very thing? This means that your divorce will

not only work for your good, it might even be a great turning point in your life.

(3) Have you thanked the Lord for your divorce? His Word tells us to give THANKS for everything (Phil. 4:6). You should thank Him for your divorce and then trust Him to use it for your good and His glory. The truth is, our God is great enough to use your divorce to lead you into a situation or blessing that might never come to pass otherwise.

• I'm thinking of a case where a precious brother was KEPT from doing something he wanted to do very badly, because he was divorced. The mission board to which he had applied turned him down. After that he devoted himself to a very specialized ministry and became quite successful. If I were to mention his name, you'd know it in a minute. It wasn't until afterwards that he saw how God used his divorce record to lead him into the work he was best suited for. The truth is, God's program is big enough to accommodate both the divorced and the non-divorced Christian. That alone should cause you to take heart.

Now I am going to suggest something that will not only make you feel easier about your divorce, but will help you become an effective servant of the Lord as well. I think you will be delighted when you hear my suggestion.

TWO THINGS YOU CAN DO:

1 Become a witness for the Lord.

The Great Commission says, "Go ye into all the world" (Mk. 16:15). You will observe that it does **not say,** "Go ye into all the CHURCH!" Therefore even if you are denied a place in some local church, it can't possibly keep you from the one task the Lord has given all of us. That's not all. To be a successful witness, one must move in the power of the Holy Spirit. Therefore you are going to find that your divorce will not keep you from being filled with the Spirit or enjoying His power. Once you begin to witness as I am going to suggest, you'll find yourself moving in the Spriit's power as never before.

Even if you are denied a place in some local church, you can still be a witness for the Lord. Witnessing to your friends at the water cooler at work can be fun when using the plan of **WITNESSING MADE EASY.**

The reason I make that suggestion is because I am in a position to equip you and train you for it. That's only one suggestion. There's something else you can do.

2 Become a private minister for the Lord.

It's true that your divorce can keep you from serving in some churches. You should know that is not true of all churches, though. There is some relaxing of the rigid stand against divorcees in some places. You might have to change your denomination to find another church that makes you feel at home. It is important that you try to find such a church, even if you have to shop around for a year or so. Why? You can't afford to be without the fellowship of other Christians. Believers cool off quickly when they try to go it alone.

Now if you can't hold a job in the church you like, don't worry about it. You can serve the Lord OUTSIDE the church, and then fellowship with the believers INSIDE the church. There's nothing wrong with that since the Great Commission takes us into the world anyway.

CAUTION: Don't let yourself become resentful toward those Christians who take a strong stand against divorce. Don't say one unkind word against them. Assume they are trying to hold a high standard in their church and this is their way of doing it. If you really want to be victorious, pray for them. Say to the Lord, "If this is the way You are leading them, then I pray You will bless them. It's their church. They have every right to run it the way they think pleases You." If you can keep that kind of an attitude, you will end up with the kind of a spirit God can use in power. It will almost guarantee the success of your private ministry.

How would you start such a ministry?

(a) Open your home to friends and acquaintences who are interested in discussing and learning the things of God. In the course of being a witness for the Lord, you are going to run into people who have no church at all. Some will be feeble Christians. Others may be people who are interested

150

in becoming Christians. If you have only one or two people who have this interest, that's plenty for a start.

If you have some new Christians and want to teach them about the Christian life, we have a really nice course of instruction called **DYNAMIC TRUTHS for the SPIRIT-FILLED LIFE.**

(b) If you have some new Christians and want to teach them the Christian life, we have a really nice course of instruction, ideally suited to the private ministry. The student text is called **"Dynamic Truths for the Spirit-filled Life."** This is an exciting series of 10 lessons that answer most of the questions plaguing new Christians, and old ones too for that matter. The teacher's book is called, **Teach Dynamic Truths.** Between these two books you'll find you have all the tools and helps necessary to do a good job in your home.

Don't shy away from these suggestions. It is easy to be a witness and to have a group meet in your home. It is fun, and you will experience the Holy Spirit's power in your life as soon as you start. Before long you'll be saying, "Every divorced Christian should know about this!"

NOTE: If you are a pastor with a divorce record, you can follow this same procedure to start a fellowship of divorced Christians. There are many who can't seem to find a church home. If the plan is successful and a number show interest, you could start a church for the benefit of those with divorces. There are a few such churches around the country and they meet a real need. So you see, a divorce can work for good for those who mean business for Christ. There is more than one way to get the job done.

The reason I am excited about the possibilities for divorced Christians is because I am in a position to help them do these things I have suggested. I know what fun it can be and I have had the joy of helping many salvage their lives and go on to do an important work for the Lord. When I say it is easy and fun, I should know . . . because . . .

THAT'S MY MINISTRY.

See that book. The title is **Witnessing Made Easy.** It contains 256 pages of witnessing know-how. It will introduce you to the **ladder-method** of witnessing. And you are going to thrill to it, especially if you tend to be shy and it is hard for you to speak to strangers about the Lord. It is a ten step plan that ASSUMES most Christians are timid at first. That's what makes it attractive to those who don't like to be thrown into a situation where they have to sink or swim.

You know about ladders, don't you?

Just as a man cannot go from the ground to the roof of his house without a ladder, neither can a Christian go from silence to active witnessing without a plan which breaks the distance up into easy steps.

Here's a man who wants to get to the roof of his house. He eyes the distance. It's at least 12 feet. Can he make it in one jump? Of course not. So what does he do? He goes and gets a ladder. He leans it against the house and what he couldn't do in one single bound, he does very easily ONE STEP AT A TIME.

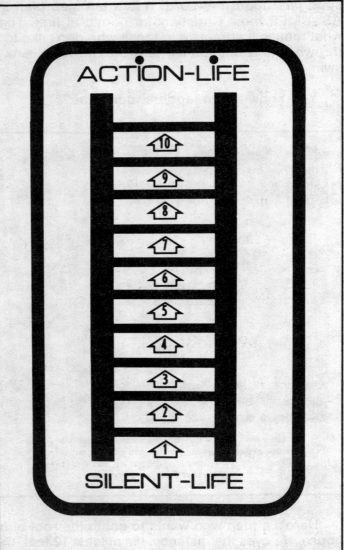

ACTION-LIFE

10
9
8
7
6
5
4
3
2
1

SILENT-LIFE

BECOMING A WITNESS IS EASIER—ONE STEP AT A TIME.

Each rung takes him that much higher until he is finally where he wants to be — on top of his house.

So it is with the ladder-method of witnessing. You are not expected to go right out and start talking to people about Jesus. You start at the bottom, in situations where you have no direct contact with people at all. Then you work your way gradually to the place where it is easy and natural for you to share your faith with others. To expect you to become a witness in ONE JUMP is ridiculous. We don't do anything else in life that way. Why should we expect to do so with the things of the Lord.

Then — as you work your way up the ladder, you learn how to use ALL the areas of your life as a witness for Jesus. It doesn't matter whether it is a trip to the store, or someone calls at your door, you're already and you know exactly what to do.

HERE'S THE FIRST STEP

If I describe the first action for you, you'll get an idea how the Lord can use such a plan to build your strengths as a witness.

We'll assume you have gone to a gas station. While the attendant is putting gas in your car, you visit the restroom. You are going to leave a tract there, but this time it will be different from anything you have done before. You go inside the restroom. "Click," you lock the door. Now there is no way for anyone to surprise you as you do the action I am about to describe. This is the ideal way to start off as a witness for the Lord — **in the world.** It's easy to testify for him in church, but out there in the world it is another story.

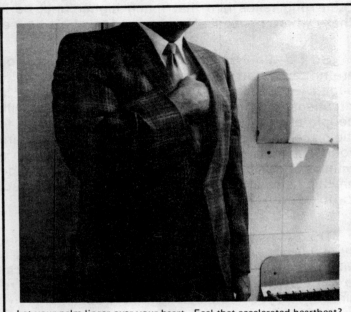

Let your palm linger over your heart. Feel that accelerated heartbeat?

Your hand reaches to your shirt pocket for a tract. But don't take it out just yet. Let your palm linger over your heart. Feel that accelerated heartbeat? Kerplump . . . kerplump . . . kerplump . . .? Why so fast? Ah — you're about to do something for Jesus in the world. That's Satan's territory! Even though the door is locked you are still in the place of fear. It's scary witnessing for the Lord — in the world.

Now you can bring out the tract. Hold it at arm's length. See it flutter? Why does it shake so? That's the trembling of your heart translated into something you can see. It's good to realize we have this fear. It's also good to know what to do about it. With your arm still outstretched, speak to the Holy Spirit. "God the Holy Spirit, behold my trembling heart and comfort me now!"

"Holy Spirit, behold my trembling heart and comfort me now!"

Look at your tract now. See — it settles down. The work of the Holy Spirit is now translated into something you can see! And what do you feel in your heart? Glorious comfort. Isn't that great! You're not through yet. Say aloud . . . **"In the name of the Lord Jesus Christ,"** and let your arm swing so that you deposit the tract on a shelf or towel box. That little exercise may seem overly simple to you, but I assure you it is a fabulous way to begin your career as a witness for Jesus. It is no small thing to have Jesus' Name on your lips in a public place.

We all have to start some place. How better than by sampling the Spirit's power in a situation that offers minimum threat. You've just seen how it is done. That's only the beginning. Imagine what the rest of the steps are like. As you climb the ladder you will learn dozens of new ways to use tracts and create witnessing opportunities. At the top of the ladder you will be able to turn almost ANY conversation into a witnessing situation. What a witness your life will become! In fact, if you want to, you can go on and learn a plan for winning souls. You'll have the strength for it. But until he climbs the ladder, there's not one Christian in a hundred who has the personality strength to present Christ to a stranger. This method of witnessing brings that kind of strength.

Say aloud..."In the name of the Lord Jesus Christ."

What you are going to like most is learning to work with the Holy Spirit — at close range. This is vital, for it is HE Who shows you how to use your life as a witness for the Lord Jesus. It is going to thrill you to watch the Spirit work right before your eyes as

158

you do the various actions described in this course. Once you begin, you'll ask yourself, "Why didn't I start this a long time ago?" Now listen to the testimony of someone who has learned the ladder-method of witnessing:

Susan Mele praises the Lord for what He has done in her life through the WITNESSING COURSE.

"When I look back to 18 months ago when I first started this course, I chuckle as I think how afraid I was of people. I can't help but praise the Lord for what He has done in my life through you people. I have never had so much fun with anything before. The real thrill has been working with the Holy Spirit. I certainly am not through. I have just begun to use my life for the Lord. Yet, I can honestly say that if I went no farther, this course was more than worthwhile for me. I have a lot of precious memories from doing the exercises since I was 'salvaged from silence!' I am recommending this course to everyone who will listen to my story!"

Susan L. Mele
13038 Dorothy Drive
Chesterland, OH 44026   (used by permission)

Isn't that terrific! I have hundreds of letters like that from people who have been lifted to a new level in Christ. Most confess they didn't realize there were so many ways to use the ordinary incidents of their daily routine for Christ. Don't you think you should send for a copy of *Witnessing Made Easy* and see what this method could do for your life? Perhaps another word of encouragement would help. Listen to the testimony of Raymond J. Weaverling, 18 Rankin Rd., Meeting House Hill, Newark, DE 17911:

Raymond Weaverling has witnessed to all his neighbors and has given out more than 3,000 tracts!

"It thrills me to look back to where I was when I first started up the ladder. Why, I was afraid to give a tract to a stranger. Even the thought of having someone see me leave a tract some place was too much for me. But the Lord has used you and this course to change all that, praise His name! I have witnessed to all my neighbors and have given out more than 3000 tracts! The fear of what people might think has left me. I never dreamed that a person could CREATE witnessing opportunities as I do now. This really is a fantastic course and I commend it to Christians everywhere!"

(used by permission)

How about it? Are you ready to let the Lord show you ways to use your life as a witness for Him? Are you ready to learn ways to witness of which you never dreamed? I hope so. Take my word for it, there is no way to know the real thrill of Christ unless we obey Him and learn how to move in the power of His Spirit. That's what makes the Christian life exciting. And the best way to begin that kind of excitement is to get active as a witness.

TWO WAYS TO GET STARTED

(1) You can order a copy of **Witnessing Made Easy.** It explains all of the techniques and describes all of the actions. (2) Or you can take the course from **Personal Christianity** with me as your personal coach. All ten lessons of the ladder-method have been prepared as a correspondence course.

NOTE: Let me way a word about the correspondence course. It is NOT a pencil/paper type. It is an ACTION course. There are specific witnessing actions you are to do, all of them in the same vein as the one I described above. After you do these actions you send me an action report. There is one for each of the 10 rungs of the ladder. You will NOT receive all ten lessons at once. You will receive two lessons at first. Then, as soon as I receive your first action report, the next lesson is mailed to you. That way you always have one lesson to work on while the other is in the mail.

There are three things to do to enroll in the course:

1. Find the application form, p. 171. Read it and fill it out. Sign it. From the information on this application a permanent record is made for you here at PC headquarters and a chart is used to plot your progress.

2. Sit down and write a letter to me telling how you KNOW you are saved. I want you to put your salvation experience on paper. To do so, ask yourself . . . **"What right do I have to call myself a born-again Christian?"** Think too about the ways you reassure yourself you are safe in the Lord. Put it all on paper, describing the best you can the mechanics of your surety in Christ. It doesn't have to be long, just factual. I am not interested in your spelling or handwriting.

Don't try to satisfy me with your statement, satisfy yourself.

This action is not as simple as it sounds. To put things of this nature on paper, a person must first process them in his mind. It often takes a lot of mental energy to reshape scattered and unfocused ideas into a solid statement, but that's what I want. If your experience in Christ is vague and shadowy, this can be a rewarding assignment. The witness-life requires a firm base. It is the launching pad from which you will go into orbit, so it must be solid.

3. Along with your application and salvation letter, enclose the enrollment fee—$10.00. You will understand this is not a money making venture when I tell you the cost of the materials for this course runs $8.38. Handling and lesson grading is not a part of that total. The purpose of this course is solely to activate saints for Christ, with the confidence that our "profit" will be laid up and waiting for the day when we will see you there!

Here are the advantages of climbing the witnessing ladder this way:

- Your work is more determined and systematic with the discipline of accounting to someone else, as reinforced by the heart-treasure principle when you invest the $10.00.

- If you are a pastor or teacher, you can systematically bring your

162

people along a step or two behind you. You can put the know-how to work in your group even as you ascend the 10 rungs of the ladder.

- Each time we receive an action report, you receive a prayer-boost by name as your report goes before the Friday night prayer-band.

- If you begin to show excessive lag in your reporting, a follow-up letter will spur you on to increased dedication.

- You receive a membership card and **permanent number** when you reach the fifth rung of the ladder. This number can be used to earn an **immediate discount** on all supplies you order from PC. In time this can return the cost of the course.

- Upon completion of the course, you receive the silver PC pin. These coveted pins are kept locked in a safe, and there is no way to secure one except by completing all ten action steps of the witnessing ladder. They truly certify the wearer to be an active and skilled witness for Christ.

- You can take your time. Some take as long as one year to complete the course. The fastest is three months. You advance to the next higher rung after you have learned to be **comfortable** witnessing at the lower level. The pressure is your own ambition to go as far as you can in Christ.

 Go to the place where you do your letter writing. Take pen and paper and get your salvation experience down in black and white. You'll enjoy sweet exhilaration doing just that much. There's a sample letter on page 170 that can serve as a guide if letter writing is hard for you. Now Satan wants you to put this off. Don't listen to him. The Holy Spirit is ready to work with you right now. As soon as you get that letter on its way to me, your faith will begin to rise. Get started as a witness and you will discover the. . .

REAL THRILL OF CHRIST!

SO DON'T CRY....!

No longer do you have to feel disqualified because you are divorced. Why? What you have just read should convince you that your divorce is not a handicap. It can be a strategic turning point in your ministry. I have shown you how that is possible. So don't feel sorry for yourself. Instead, rejoice that the Holy Spirit is ready to use you in ways you might have never considered before. A whole new life of service opens before you and you'll find your divorce can be a definite advantage when you look to the Lord rather than your circumstances.

Isn't it wonderful to know that God can use your divorce for His glory? Sure it is. Once you get active and start up the witnessing ladder, you will be thrilled to look back over the steps and see how He has used you. That will make you praise Him all the more. And here's what is so fabulous. You will find that you are even more effective for Christ now than had the divorce never occurred at all! Isn't that precious! It is to the glory of our God that He can take even our mistakes and turn them to good. There is no way to miss when you set yourself to serve our wonderful Lord Jesus.

Isn't He fantastic!

PRINCIPLES BASIC TO
THE MATTER OF DIVORCE

Here are listed the biblical principles encountered thus far in considering: (1) God's heart, (2) the Law, (3) man's sinful condition. Together, they nearly resolve the divorce difficulty upon a single reading:

1. The letter of the Law is a vehicle which carries the message of the Law.

2. The letter of the Law (actual wording) becomes a **killer** when imposed upon sinful men who cannot keep it (2 Cor. 3:6).

3. The only escape for man under the Law is through the death of Christ.

4. God is a Father, not a Lawyer. When the **purpose** of the Law is better served, God will tolerate an evil to

keep His Law from producing a greater evil.

   a. Samuel's trip to Bethlehem (I Sam. 16).

   b. The divine honoring of Rahab's lie (Jos. 2; Heb. 11:31).

   c. Jesus' freeing of the woman taken in adultery (John 8).

   d. Jesus' picking corn on the Sabbath (Mk. 2:23-28).

   e. Jesus' reference to David's eating of the Shewbread to teach the heart obedience principle (Mk. 2:25).

   f. God's own command to slay entire nations in direct opposition to the Sixth Commandment (I Sam. 15:3).

5. Real obedience to God's Law is from the heart (Rom. 6:16,17).

   a. Adultery is committed within the heart (Matt. 5:28).

   b. Murder is in the heart (I John 3:15). Physical murder is merely hatred in action.

6. God looks upon the **heart** of an individual to behold his obedience, while man's vision is limited only to **external representations.**

7. No man, other than Jesus, has ever been able to **fulfill** even one of the commandments of the Law.

8. Christians err when they apply the LETTER OF EITHER TESTAMENT against each other as a standard or measuring rod of personal righteousness.

STEP ONE: Should you consider a separation?

> Separation can be helpful. It allows emotions to die down so that you can make a sane evaluation of your marriage. Be sure to ask yourself the three questions on page 102.

STEP TWO: Is the marriage making you bitter or better?

> The marital pressures will either make you like Christ or like Satan. If you find yourself changing into the likeness of Satan, then the marriage is worse than divorce. If you are becoming sweeter and more like Jesus, then the marriage is better than divorce.

STEP THREE: Make the decision.

> As soon as you determine what your marriage is really doing to you (bitter or better), make your decision. Don't be afraid to do so because you are going to test the decision before you carry it out.

STEP FOUR: Test the decision before the Lord.

> Take your decision to the Lord in prayer. Frankly tell Him this is what **you feel is best.** Then wait. Sleep on it two or even three nights. God will grant you peace or a godly fear in your heart as His way of showing you His will. He will be communicating His OWN feelings via your feelings. Watch for Satan, though, he will try to confuse you. If you don't toss and turn with anxiety, but can sleep well, that's the peaceful indication. If you are torn apart with frustration, that's the fearful indication.

STEP FIVE: Carry out your decision by faith.

Once you know God's will, carry out your decision boldly. If you have elected to stay, praise God for your trials and let them produce their fruit in your life. Stop all complaining from that day on. If you elect to leave, do so resolutely—**"as unto the Lord."** Ignore comments or criticism from others and keep your eyes on Jesus. Satan will try to use your friends to torment you and hurt you. Give thanks to God for your situation whichever choice you make.

To take the course

1. Fill out the application on page 171.
2. Prepare the statement of your salvation experience. Sample letter on next page.
3. Enclose your check or money order.
4. Expect your first lesson in about 10 days.

We furnish everything

COMPLETE COST $10.00

This includes:

☆ Copy of your text WITNESSING MADE EASY
☆ Assorted tracts for assignments
☆ Witness pins
☆ Witnessing pen and DASH WARNING SIGN
☆ Pocket plastic tract holder
☆ Booklets and dailog cards
☆ Lesson sheets and action report forms
☆ Maintenance of your individual file
☆ Lifted to Jesus by name in prayer group
☆ Completion certificate and silver PC pin
☆ Numbered membership card giving you 10% discount on purchases at PC

Graduation means

- You have traveled from silence to outspokenness for Christ

- You have learned the skill of working with the Holy Spirit

- You have learned how to create a witnessing situation

- You have overcome fear and embarrassment by action

SAMPLE LETTER

Date _____

Dear brother Lovett,

I have been studying **"The Compassionate Side of Divorce."**
I want to be a witness for our Lord Jesus. My application and
photo are enclosed. And here is my experience in Christ:

"I know that I am saved because..."

INSTRUCTIONS

Complete your letter in a paragraph or two and don't worry about
the following:

1. Spelling
2. Handwriting, though I do have to read it. Typewriter would be
   helpful if you have one.
3. Grammar or sentence structure
4. Lack of education
5. What I think of the letter as to style. I am interested only in your
   experience.

HINTS

1. Do you have a favorite text on which you rest your salvation?
2. Is there a date or event which you can recall when you opened
   your heart to Jesus?
3. Are there ways in which you reestablish your heart when doubts
   strike?
4. Review in your mind the actual transaction which takes place
   when one receives the Lord. Can you mention something of the
   mechanics?

I am glad we can become personal friends, brother Lovett. And I
look forward to receiving the lessons and coaching helps. I will be
faithful to ask the Holy Spirit to work with us on this program and
help me to become a vigorous witness for our Lord Jesus as the
know-how comes into my life.

Eagerly in Christ,

Signed _____

WITNESSING COURSE
BY CORRESPONDENCE
APPLICATION

PERSONAL CHRISTIANITY
Box 549
Baldwin Park, Calif. 91706 (213) 338-7333

> photo or
> snapshot

Date _____

Full Name _____

Complete Address _____

City, State, Zip _____

Minister __ Teacher __ Layman __ Housewife __ Student __

Name of your church _____

Your occupation _____

Do you receive a copy of PERSONAL CHRISTIANITY regularly? _____

I want to be a witness for our Lord Jesus. I hereby apply for the action course you offer. Enclosed is $10.00 to cover the cost of the lessons and materials needed for the assignments.

Check one below:

My salvation experience letter is enclosed _____

You already have my salvation letter _____

As the Lord strengthens my witness-life, I grant PERSONAL CHRISTIANITY permission to use my testimony for the purpose of strengthening other Christians.

Signed _____

Brother Lovett was saved through his "accidental" attendance at a minister's conference where he eavesdropped the conversation of a group of nationally known Christian leaders. There he overheard a discussion on the mechanics of salvation. For years he had been under conviction, yet no one troubled to introduce him to Christ. Armed with the necessary insight for the salvation experience, he hurried home to share it with his wife, Marjorie.

Together they knelt and invited Christ to come into their hearts.

A graduate of California Baptist Theological Seminary, he holds the M.A. and B.D. degrees conferred Magna Cum Laude. He has completed graduate work in Psychology at Los Angeles State College and holds an honorary doctorate from the Protestant Episcopal University in London. He is a retired Air Force Chaplain with the rank of Lt. Colonel.

Pastor Lovett is the author of the books and tools produced by Personal Christianity. Able to express the profound things of God in simple, practical language, his writings strengthen Christians the world over. The advent of his "Soul-Winning Made Easy," has drastically changed evangelism methods in America, while the anti-satan skill offered in his "Dealing with the Devil," has alerted multitudes to their authority over our enemy through Christ. Dr. Lovett's experience as an editor of the Amplified New Testament and a director of the foundation which produced it, prompted him to begin work on the Personal New Testament Commentary.

PERSONAL CHRISTIANITY IS ..

A local church with a literature ministry.

We are incorporated under the Laws of the State of California as a local church.

We not only provide a worship center for the residents of the area, but exist as a "ministry of helps" [1 Cor 12:28] toward the "Body of Christ."

PC is not affiliated with any denomination, organization or council of churches.

God has given PC the task of producing the spiritual mechanics for personal obedience to the Great Commission and maturity in the Christian life. Unique, know-how tools are developed within the church and made available to God's people everywhere. Our outreach is by means of the U.S. Postal system which makes possible *personal contact* with individuals and churches across the land and throughout the world.

We bear the name PERSONAL CHRISTIANITY because we seek to involve people personally with the Lord Jesus, the Holy Spirit and the Great Commission.

All who care about Christ are welcome to worship with us. Those further interested in "equipping Christians for action," are invited to invest their talents and strengths with ours. We are interested in every Christian and church willing to take a vigorous stand for Christ in these gloomy days.

175